Passive Income Ideas 2022

*Tried-and-True Methods to Generate a
Steady Stream of Income Online Even if
You're a Complete Newbie
(Crash Course for Beginners)*

Bert Dennis

Table of Contents

Introduction

That is the question you must answer: to dropship or not to dropship.

When deciding to establish a dropshipping business, every entrepreneur asks themselves this question. Many people will tell you that this business concept is a hoax and that you will never make any money if you pursue it.

You are the captain of your own ship, and you must make an educated decision on how to launch your company. This is why this book sets out to walk you through the essentials step by step as a novice, so you may build your business calmly and methodically. Your goal is success, which you will attain by following the counsel given and getting off on the right foot, despite the naysayers' doomsday forecasts and unwanted negative advice.

So let's get started with all you need to know and understand about starting a dropshipping business with the least amount of hassle.

Chapter One: Start From The Beginning

Starting off on the proper foot and knowing the answers to all of the vital questions is critical to your success. It's considerably easier to get it right from the start than it is to go back and fix problems later because you were impatient or tried to take shortcuts.

What Is Dropshipping and How Does It Work?

Dropshipping is an e-commerce business concept that varies from traditional e-commerce in that you do not physically handle or stockpile the things you sell. You can create an e-commerce store on your own website or through platforms like Shopify, Amazon, or eBay.

You offer your clients particular products that are available from reputable wholesale suppliers and manufacturers who specialise in your chosen sector, and the chain reaction begins when your client places an order with you.

Your supplier, in turn, places an order with you. Your supplier bills you for the product at the agreed-upon price and then ships it directly to your customer.

Your suppliers could be located anywhere in the planet, depending on your unique items. There are no restrictions on where your suppliers are situated; this is especially useful for sensitive products, as the period between manufacture and delivery to the client is decreased because inventory is not sitting on a shelf hoping to be sold before it expires.

When you choose to establish a business using the dropshipping business model, it transforms the way you do business and gives you a lot of flexibility in your everyday operations.

It's Critical to Have the Right Mentality

To be successful in your dropshipping business, you must develop a strong entrepreneurial mindset from the beginning. You can't go into starting your own business with apathy and a don't give a damn attitude. If you do, you are putting yourself in a position to fail. You must be hungry for success and enter this business with a can-do attitude and determination.

Commitment

You must totally commit to this business effort and make use of all available resources. The best part is that you don't have to give up your day job to start your dropshipping business; you don't have to choose between the two. You can juggle how you manage client inquiries and orders around your other work if you are dedicated. This allows you to start your company and allow it to flourish until you are ready to make the full transition to running it. You will reap the benefits of having a smoothly operating firm that requires less effort to maintain once it gathers pace if you completely commit from the start.

Perseverance

We all live in an instant world where we anticipate rapid pleasure for everything from food and entertainment to finances and purchases. We've grown accustomed to acquiring anything with the click of a mouse or the press of a button. Unfortunately, many people have developed a spoiled and petulant attitude as a result of this, which does not foster strong character, devotion, or endurance.

Your ability to persevere is crucial to your success. There are numerous quotes and proverbs regarding perseverance, not giving up, and trying again if you don't succeed the first time. There is a reason for these sayings; they indicate that you are not the first person to face challenges or problems, and they were coined by people who endured and tried until they found exactly what worked for them. Perseverance leads to determination, which leads to a greater desire to achieve, which is exactly what you need to start your own dropshipping business. You just keep going until each facet of your business fits neatly into place, even if things don't fall into place right away.

No-Quick-Fix Mentality

When it comes to starting your own business, there are no easy cures. Attempting to skip critical processes in order to save time and effort can only lead to failure. Do not be fooled by get-rich-quick schemes that promise you a million-dollar income with no effort on your part; such schemes do not exist. Get rid of any fast fix mentality you may have; it will only cause you to waste money, and skipping important processes at the starting phase of your firm will be costly to rectify afterwards. Do things correctly from the start and develop a strong foundation for your dropshipping business that will be able to withstand setbacks and challenges as they arise.

Invest your time and effort

Although the words "blood, sweat, and tears" may sound unnecessarily dramatic, you must devote your time and efforts to make your dropshipping business a success. People are far too quick to put significant sums of money into a company enterprise; there is no reason to do so. Dropshipping allows you to start your own business with little money and effort by investing yourself and using your energy to get it off the ground.

This type of investment has numerous advantages that will benefit you in the long run as your company expands.

- As you get direct understanding of how each aspect of your organisation runs, your abilities and knowledge will increase along with it. Money can't buy the abilities you'll gain about running a business. When you start expanding, you'll gain a better understanding of how each department of the business operates, which will help you manage the individuals you hire.
- You will have a better understanding of your clients, including how they think and what they desire. Markets are constantly evolving, and by becoming a hands-on part of the company's operations, you'll learn about market trends and how to keep your consumers satisfied. This will enable you to make judgments about which providers to hire and how to market your website to persuade potential clients to utilise your services.

When you are intimately involved in the day-to-day operations of your firm, you understand what to spend money on that is critical to its success. Your priorities move away from non-essentials that may appear good or devices that you can easily do without when your thinking shifts.

Concentrate on solutions rather than problems.

We frequently focus so intently on a problem that we become so engrossed in the minutiae of the problem that we lose sight of the bigger picture. Instead of thinking, "I have a problem, I don't know what to do," change your perspective to, "I have to find a solution to this problem."

Train your mind to see things from a solution perspective rather than a problem perspective. Instead of stressing, explore all of your options for finding solutions. Knowledge is literally at your fingertips thanks to the internet. Start looking for new providers if you're having trouble with one. Find out what's accessible on Amazon, eBay, and Shopify, and how you can use these platforms to your advantage to address the problem you're having. People offer information and advise on how they solved their challenges on a variety of blogs devoted to dropshipping. The answers are out there; all you have to do is take the time to look for the best options that meet your requirements.

Mistakes should be viewed as a learning opportunity rather than a failure.

Blunders are not the end of the world; no one on the earth can claim to have lived a life without making any mistakes. In every form of business, mistakes are bound to occur. However, how you deal with the mistake and what you do about it makes a big difference.

A blunder does not automatically imply that you are a complete failure who should shut down your new dropshipping business. Every blunder is an opportunity to learn. You'll learn how to come up with answers and other strategies to avoid making the same mistake again in the future.

Mistakes give you valuable customer service lessons. You learn to admit your mistakes and how to calm down upset consumers without losing them.

Every customer service problem you deal with improves your customer service skills and benefits you in the long run.

A supplier error allows you to enhance your abilities in cooperation and negotiation, which benefits both your business and your supplier's business.

Chapter Two: Reasons Why You Should Start a Dropshipping Business

Is Your Time and Effort Really Worth It?

The answer is an emphatic yes. You will not receive a stress-free means to earn income, just as you will not get a stress-free approach to establish any form of business. You'll have to put in a lot of effort and dedication to your business. You can anticipate the end result to reflect the amount of effort and time you're willing to put into it.

All businesses must face the truth that we now work in a world that has changed dramatically over the last few decades. Strategies that worked 30 years ago are no longer relevant, and if you want to be competitive and profitable, you must adapt and expand to keep up with how technological advancements have changed how people shop.

People no longer want to have to physically go to stores and be limited to what they can find there. Everyone has a limited amount of time and wants to get as much done as possible in a day, so shopping on a smartphone or laptop is significantly more convenient.

As the globe markets move faster, e-commerce has taken over the world, and the dropshipping business model fits very nicely. People nowadays want to shop online and have their products delivered to them directly, therefore the retail behemoths of the past are struggling. This is understandable given that ecommerce has made worldwide buying accessible to consumers.

The gloomy truth that traditional retailers face is depicted in this figure given by Business Insider and correlated from data within their firm. The graph clearly demonstrates why starting your own dropshipping business is worthwhile.

Chapter Three: Benefits of The Dropshipping Business Model

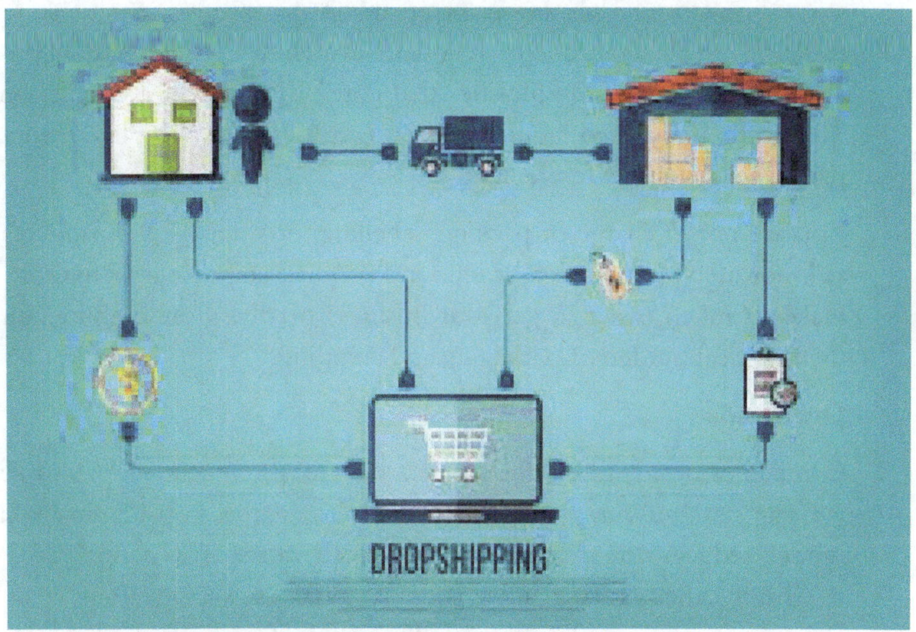

Dropshipping differs from traditional retail shops in that it does not function from a physical location, which drastically affects how it operates. Dropshipping is also distinct from traditional e-commerce in that it purchases inventory and ships orders to customers from that inventory.

Dropshipping has a long list of advantages that are unique to the dropshipping business model.

Less Investment in Capital

Yes, money is required to start a firm. The main distinction is that you don't need a lot of money to get started with dropshipping.

You merely require some cash as a safety net while you strive to get your business up and running. All businesses have small operating costs, and you should keep in mind that you'll need to budget for site hosting and any fees associated with using dropshipping platforms. It's a good idea to keep some cash on hand for unexpected expenses. Keeping this in mind will reduce stress and allow you to concentrate on getting your company off the ground.

Easy to Get Started

Because you don't have any physical stock, you don't need a warehouse to store inventory. This means you won't have any warehouse-related expenses, such as property rental or warehouse equipment. This also eliminates all of the complexities that come with warehouse management. There are no wasted hours reordering product or keeping meticulous records of inventory movement.

You are not in charge of packing, labelling, or shipping the products you sell, nor are you in charge of inbound product shipments or returns. This makes it much easier to get your business off the ground and eliminates the logistical burden of packaging and shipping.

Overheads

Companies deal with overheads on a daily basis, which is a pain. Because you can start and run your business from home, the dropshipping business model reduces the majority of overhead costs. It's natural for your overhead expenses to rise as your business grows, but your costs will always be lower than those of a traditional retail location.

Location

With a dropshipping business, you have the most flexibility in terms of location, and you can literally run your business from anywhere with an internet connection. You don't need a fancy office to impress potential customers; all you need is a laptop and access to the internet, which is excellent because you can conduct business whether you're sitting at a desk at home or on the road.

The International Market

You have access to markets all over the world with e-commerce and the dropshipping business model; you are not confined to local products in your nation. Dropshipping is possible from any supplier or manufacturer in the world. Customers appreciate this since they have access to a much larger selection than would be available from any local business.

This graph depicts the enormous global popularity of e-commerce.

You may easily access global markets for your dropshipping business via online retail platforms.

(n.d., MGR Consulting Group)

Availability of a Wide Range of Products in Your Specialty

Niche products can limit your options for what products you can add to your e-commerce store because only a few suppliers may supply the items you require. If you were only allowed to sell to local markets, you'd have a lot of challenges, limit your business's growth, and hurt your profit margin. Access to worldwide markets is a game changer for niche items, making it a top benefit for all niche product vendors.

Substantial Risk Factors Are Reduced

Dropshipping, as opposed to the more traditional e-commerce business model, has a significant advantage in terms of minimising the risk of financial loss to the dropshipping seller, since you do not risk not being able to sell the goods you have already paid for. The only monetary loss if you encounter a quiet period and don't make a sale is the potential profit you could have made on a transaction.

Another risk-reducing feature is that you only place an order with your supplier after your customer has placed and paid for an order with you.

When you contact your supplier, you use the money that has already been paid to you rather than your own money, so you don't have to always make sure you have additional funds when placing an order with your supplier.

A win-win situation for both the supplier and the dropshipping company

Suppliers and manufacturers want to cooperate with dropshipping companies because the more people who sell their items, the more money they make overall. Even while dropshipping businesses do not buy his items in bulk, suppliers are eager to negotiate a better or wholesale price with them.

Their enthusiasm stems from the fact that they gain more exposure for their items while incurring no marketing costs, as well as having more time to develop their goods. Suppliers are well aware that establishing a positive relationship with a dropshipping firm ensures that the company will return to them for more products at a reasonable price.

With a more productive supplier and a loyal dropshipping firm that keeps a regular flow of orders coming in, this is a win-win situation for everyone, resulting in increased profit for both the supplier and the dropshipping company.

Taking Advantage of Online Retail Platforms

Making use of online retail platforms is crucial to the success of your dropshipping company. We'll go into the specifics of online retail platforms in later chapters, but for now, let's look at the big picture.

Unlimited Customer Exposure

Every online business wants to reach out to as many potential clients as possible. When you join one of the online retail platforms, you gain instant access to an almost limitless number of clients without having to spend a lot of money on marketing.

A Wide Range of Products in Your Niche to Choose From

Another significant advantage of using online retail platforms is the vast array of products available that fall within your niche; you can pick and choose what you think best suits you, and if a particular product does not sell well, you can easily switch to another product on the site. When you use retail platforms, experimenting with which products sell the best is not a costly venture because you don't lose money on inventory that isn't selling. Keeping track of your sales patterns allows you to pivot and alter quickly in order to stay on top of your game.

Countless Vacant Niches

Amazon, Shopify, and eBay, for example, always offer a significant number of vacant niches for you to investigate, providing you with a perfect opportunity to develop your business into other niches. The retail platforms handle the legwork, and your firm profits without you having to spend manhours and labour looking for new prospects.

Scaling

What does scaling mean in the context of a dropshipping business, and how does it work?

This is one of the most common questions posed by entrepreneurs who want to establish their own dropshipping business.

Growing and extending your dropshipping business is part of scaling up. Scaling this business model is far easier than scaling a typical e-commerce business because the old business model entails a lot more effort; the more orders received, the more work there is.

The method is different for a dropshipping business. Your dropshipping suppliers do the majority of the work required to process more orders, making the process easier for you and removing the majority of the increasing difficulties experienced by other businesses.

Chapter Four: Drawbacks To Be Aware Of

Business models have pros and cons, it is the same with the dropshipping model. This does not mean it is a bad business model, simply that you should be aware of drawbacks that are specific to dropshipping. You make allowances for the drawbacks, try to avoid those you can and find solutions around problems wherever possible. Facing drawbacks does not mean your business is a failure, you can overcome many drawbacks by planning ahead and putting backup solutions in place.

Margins Are Low

Many people are put off by the low margins in their chosen niche. People want to see higher profits and grow their business faster. If you are prepared to start small, persevere, and get to know everything about operating a dropshipping business in the very competitive field of e-commerce, you will grow steadily and reap the benefits of your hard work.

Competition in the Market Place

E-commerce in very competitive and sellers undercut each other to make money faster. Dropshipping companies are easy to set up with a small cash startup, making it a very competitive business model. The best way to deal with this is by starting up your business correctly, give quality service to your customers, and use all the resources available to you to develop a good business reputation.

Issues with Inventory and Product Fulfillment

As a dropshipping business model, you do not control your own inventory and you are not able to keep track of the flow of stock. You depend on suppliers and wholesalers that service many other merchants as well. This can create issues with products being out of stock when you place your order.

Your suppliers are in charge of product fulfillment and mistakes and delays in shipping can occur. You will have to deal with your irate customers, so it is wise to develop as many backup supplies as you can to accommodate your customers with alternative products.

Online Retail Platforms

Online retail platforms are a great benefit for dropshipping companies, but it can also be a drawback as customers can go around you and purchase the same products directly on the retail platforms.

Shipping Can Become Complex

Dropshipping companies normally source their products through several different suppliers and wholesalers. Shipping to customers can become complex with multiple item orders that are sourced from more than one supplier. You then will have a separate shipping charge for each item of the multiple product order, and you cannot pass the extra costs on to your customer, you will have to bear the extra costs. This cuts into your profit margin.

Suppliers Can Make Mistakes

Suppliers make mistakes and when that happens you will be blamed. The responsibility is yours as the customer put the order in with you, not with your supplier. Supplier mistakes can be for various reasons, some legitimate mistakes, others caused by problems within the supplier's own company.

To minimize mistakes of shoddy workmanship, below standard packing materials, and shipments being damaged or lost, you have to source your suppliers carefully. Should suppliers let you down through negligence, you should switch to a reputable supplier immediately as these mistakes reflect badly on you. Your business reputation is incredibly important and you do not want to damage this.

Scaling Abilities of Suppliers

Not all suppliers are equally competent and some may not have the ability to keep up with scaling as your company grows. The great news is that you have access to suppliers around the world as well as the online retail platforms to source your products, so it is very easy to switch suppliers.

Chapter Five: Different Forms Of Dropshipping

The dropshipping business model started out very basic. It was more of a service than a full business model where product manufacturers and wholesale companies offered a dropshipping service to suppliers. The suppliers would then ship products to customers one by one as and when customers placed an order for a specific product.

The dropshipping business model evolved from that to where dropshipping has become a standalone complete business. We now have several forms of the dropshipping business model with variations as per the needs of individual businesses.

From Suppliers

This is the most personal form of the dropshipping business model where interaction with the suppliers is by phone and email. Terms and contracts, interactions with the support team, all the negotiations are done with real people, not with automated systems.

Benefits

Sustainable business

Building business relationships with suppliers creates a maintainable business that is long term. With this form of dropshipping, your supplier is much more approachable and accommodating when problems pop up or when new products come online. Many dropshipping companies prefer this type of dropshipping as they are more comfortable with personal relationships than the anonymity of using the e-commerce online retail platforms.

Mutual Interests

It is normal for any business to experience problems and having a personal relationship with a supplier changes how problems are resolved.

It is to the mutual benefit of the supplier and the dropshipping company to work together to resolve problems in a positive way. It is not simply a case of you losing a sale and making no profit. The supplier is aware of the impact each lost sale has on his own business.

Drawbacks

Difficult to Find

When you use online retail platforms everything is impersonal, you approach any of the large number of online platforms that is easily available on the internet. When you use suppliers you have to put in a lot of work to find a supplier you can fully trust, who is professional and reliable. Should anything happen to your supplier, you are left in limbo until you can source another reliable supplier.

Human Error

Human error can spell disaster for a dropshipping company. Suppliers who are not vigilant and maintain tight control over their inventory could have far reaching consequences for you and the reputation of your business.

When an e-commerce order is placed it constitutes a binding legal contract between you as the seller and your customer. It is deemed completely unprofessional for a seller to cancel an order and will result in a negative by the customer on your website and on social media. When this happens, the dropshipping seller tries to avoid this and, as an emergency measure, place an order for the specific item on one of the online retail platforms or an alternative supplier, most often at a higher price. You have to inform your customer of the delay in shipping their order, which could cause the loss of a return customer.

Relationships are difficult to maintain.

If you decide to use suppliers for your dropship business, you'll need to keep in constant contact with them. You won't be able to establish a strong working relationship with your suppliers if you only communicate with them via phone, email, and whatever chat apps they use. This takes time, and some people are put off by it. They prefer the fast, automated communication that online retail platforms provide.

Creating a Store on an E-Commerce Platform

The simplest and quickest way to get your dropshipping business up and running is to use an online retail platform. It's important to understand that not all online retail platforms are created equal. Each platform has its own set of guidelines and policies. You should research each of these platforms to determine which one meets all of your specific requirements and is the most cost-effective for your dropshipping business.

Timeline for Setup

The big retail platforms promise to have your business up and running in as little as 24 hours, which is a huge plus. The majority of first-time entrepreneurs are still trying to find their footing in their business venture and lack the skills and tools to do it on their own. As a result, seeing their store and being able to organise and sell in such a short period of time is really important to them.

Audience in the Near Future

Instead of laboriously establishing up their own website and working to achieve a decent search engine rating, they have immediate access to a large audience in their niche. Inexperienced dropshipping business owners may find e-commerce intimidating, as most begin with an idea they hope to turn into a profitable venture. Your chosen specialisation may be fantastic, but the complexities of the process can be intimidating. Having access to everything that the retail platforms have to offer makes getting started with dropshipping much easier.

Marketing

Unless you are a seasoned professional marketer, marketing may be a nightmare for most people. Outsourcing your company's marketing is expensive, and it eats up any funds you have set aside, money that could be better spent on other elements of your company. Signing up with an online retail platform of your choice relieves you of the enormous load of marketing.

Possibilities for Apps and Automation

Dropshipping from online platforms gives you access to a big number of apps that you wouldn't be able to get for free or at a low cost if you had to buy them for your own dropshipping website. E-commerce is primarily reliant on apps, and in today's competitive marketplaces, several apps are required to run a successful firm.

Drawbacks

Many of the disadvantages of selling through retail platforms are unique to each of them. However, there are several common negatives that impair your cash flow, are time demanding, and can severely effect your organisation.

Various Fees

When you dropship through retail portals, there are a number of fees to consider, and they can add up quickly. Depending on how the unique retail platform runs, some platforms have higher fees.

The following are some of the fees to be aware of:

Subscription fees can vary depending on the plan you select and the benefits of those plans.

Fees for listing a home. Fees for determining the final value of a home (eBay).

There is no true individuality.

Your store's appearance, marketing, and branding are all at the authority of the online retail site. Individuality and customization are not possible.

There is no contact with customers.

You don't create rapport with clients since you don't communicate with them on a personal level. To them, you're just a virtual e-commerce store on a computer screen. Customers believe they owe you no loyalty or consideration since you don't create long-term relationships with them.

Not Investing in Assets

Your company is a valuable asset in which you have invested time, effort, and money. When you dropship through suppliers and your own website, your company becomes an asset with a market worth if you ever decide to sell it. When you close your account, your online store on the retail platforms ceases to exist.

Dropshipping by Arbitrage

Dropshipping has been in the headlines a lot lately, and it's a hot topic of discussion. Arbitrage selling is not permitted on online retail platforms. To choose this type of dropshipping, you must first grasp how it varies from others and all of the advantages and disadvantages that come with arbitrage selling.

Arbitrage dropshipping is the practise of pitting one retail platform against another. Arbitrage merchants do not find suppliers and display the products in their stores on the retail platform.

Platform A, for example, sells a product for $10, but Platform B sells the identical item at a higher price. On Platform A, the arbitrage seller purchases the product at a lower price and supplies the buyer's delivery address on Platform B. Platform A then provides the product to the customer of Platform B. The difference between the lower and higher prices advertised is pocketed by the arbitrage dropshipper.

Benefits

Numerous Vendors

There will be several providers on the retail platform listing the same products for the bulk of things available through e-commerce, yet prices will vary from supplier to seller. This means you may simply swap providers based on who has the precise goods you're looking for at any given time. You keep your consumers satisfied because they don't have to wait for stock or a delivery delay.

There will be no delay in entering the market.

Everything you require is already present. Setting up a website and cultivating connections with vendors takes very little effort. Simply compare the costs of specific things across the various shopping platforms, and you can begin collecting orders.

Automation

Most areas of your business can run automatically once you've set up shop, giving you with more than enough time to provide excellent customer service, thanks to the wide range of automation technologies available.

Drawbacks/Sustainability

Dropshipping in its form is not a long-term viable business model. The ease with which anyone may start a dropshipping business draws a significant number of people looking to make as much money as possible in the quickest amount of time. Profit margins are diminishing as a result of the strong competition. This means that in order to break even, you must seek to sell more and more. There is no room for cancelled orders or delivery issues with such a narrow profit margin since you simply do not have the cash flow to deal with these issues.

Without automation, this would not be possible.

The competition in this type of dropshipping is so strong that it's no longer feasible to do so without utilising every available sort of automation. You're up against not only other enterprises in your specialty, but also bulk merchants that offer thousands of products, some of which will include your specialised products. Everyone is jumping on the bandwagon, and there is only so much money to go around, therefore individual gains are dwindling.

Not in Retail Platforms' Best Interests

Arbitrage dropshipping has sparked debate among online retail platforms, as it has a negative influence on their customer base. The platforms aren't opposed to the dropshipping business model, but they are opposed to arbitrage dropshipping, which pits one platform against another. Customers are aware that there is a flood of persons engaged in arbitrage selling.

Customers become suspicious when their product from Platform B arrives in Platform A packaging. They then switch to a different platform for their online purchases in the future.

Taking use of Amazon's Fulfillment Service

Dropshipping is permissible on Amazon, but the traditional practise of dropshipping is discouraged. Dropshipping enterprises have always gotten their products from suppliers who specialise in their niche.

The supplier is responsible for physically handling the products, and he or she also handles storage, packaging, and shipping.

The dropshipping firm must purchase minimum order sizes from the original supplier using the FBA system, and it is then stored in one of Amazon's warehouses. Instead of the original supplier from whom you purchased the merchandise, Amazon becomes your dropshipper.

By taking over the activities that a supplier would normally execute, the FBA system provides various benefits to the dropshipping company. As an Amazon reseller, you'll have access to all of the services and resources available to all Amazon shop owners, as well as being a part of the world's most famous brand.

For many entrepreneurs, the dropshipping concept is intimidating. They must invest in inventory and incur several costs they may not be financially prepared for when they are just starting out, rather than the usual dropshipping model with modest startup costs.

The full details, costs, and policies for using the Fulfilled by Amazon dropshipping business model may be found in Chapter 10.

Chapter Six: Find Your Niche

If you want to run a successful dropshipping business, you can't afford to provide a vast range of products. The rivalry from retailers, other e-commerce enterprises, and online shopping platforms is simply too intense.

What Exactly Is a Niche?

You must specialise and focus on a single product or specialty, and you must only sell things that fall into that area. It is just not financially viable for a dropshipping company to scrounge around for things that capture the eye or a trendy trend at the time.

Determining a topic to focus in among the nearly countless niches available globally can be difficult, and for anyone new to the dropshipping business model, settling on one specific niche to specialise in can feel overwhelming.

We'll walk you through the best rules for finding the niche that's suitable for you.

What do you care about and what piques your interest?

Make a list of things you're enthusiastic about, things that pique your interest, and that would be a good fit for your dropshipping business. It is critical to select a specialty with which you can identify. You must be familiar with the product and be able to sell with confidence to customers, knowing that you will be able to provide competent advice if they have questions.

If you are passionate about the area you chose, you will be more perseverant and determined to achieve, even if difficulties arise. It will be considerably easier to quit at the first bump in the road if you don't care about the things you offer.

Many dropshipping businesses began as a pastime for the owner, which grew into a thriving business where products are sold to people with similar interests.

Your success hinges on your ability to conduct research.

It's one thing to be enthusiastic and informed about the niche you want to enter, but you're also beginning a business. You must conduct extensive study to establish if your chosen niche will generate an income stream for you.

Examine the Best Products in Your Field

Search for the products you wish to sell in your dropshipping business on websites like ClickBank, Simple Goods, and Selify, for example. The more of your specialised products you can discover on the market, the better, as it indicates a need.

If none of your niche items are available on these websites, it means your niche products aren't in demand and haven't been successfully monetized by someone else.

Google Apps

To find keywords and keyword combinations related to your specialty, use Google Keyword Planner and Google Trends. Google tools will tell you how frequently your keywords are searched in search engines. You can use Google tools to research and determine the demand for your niche products by looking at what people are searching for.

Google Patterns examines variations in the amount of online searches over time and analyses trends in those searches. Google Trends statistics reveal any seasonal trends for the product search phrases you used. This provides you a decent idea of whether your lovely products will have periods of great demand and then slow down at other times of the year, indicating that your niche product income will fluctuate.

Google Trends also provides information on the locations from which searches for keywords related to your specialised products are made.

The Internet and Social Media

When it comes to deciding which specialty will work best for you, social media is quite powerful. Check out what's being said about your specialty on Facebook, how people are talking about it, and look for groups and forums.

Costs of Shipping

Your profit margin is heavily influenced by shipping costs. If it's too high, your markup will drive up your selling prices too much, causing potential clients to hunt for cheaper alternatives elsewhere. If you can absorb the delivery costs rather than passing them along with a significant markup in price, low shipping prices can be used as a marketing strategy and promotional tool. Customers will notice free delivery right away, which will lead to a boost in sales.

Profitability Margin

It's critical to remember that the amount of effort required to sell a low-cost item is identical to the effort required to promote a high-cost item. It is thus worthwhile to seek out a niche with high-end products, as this will increase your overall profit margin.

Dimensions and Weight

People sometimes overlook the physical size and weight of the products they intend to sell when opting to establish a dropshipping business. Shipping charges are inconvenient, and everyone tries to avoid them as much as possible. This is critical because if your chosen niche products have high shipping costs, your profits can rapidly vanish like mist.

Marketing for Lawyers

Make thorough research about the things you wish to offer and ensure that you will not face any legal issues. You must be able to offer your niche products in any location. It's critical that you can sell on online retail platforms, your own website, and on social media without fear of being shut down for violating any state or foreign laws.

Impulse Purchasers

A large percentage of internet customers see something they like and decide to buy it on the spur of the moment. People's purchasing habits have altered as a result of having the entire world of shopping at their fingertips. This should be considered while choosing your specialty, and the things you sell should appeal to impulse shoppers.

You immediately broaden your consumer base by selling things that appeal to impulse buyers. True, the majority of impulse consumers do not become repeat clients. When you sum up the amount of money you make from these kind of sales over time, you'll be astonished at how much it adds up to.

Develop a Personal Interest Strategy

When you are truly passionate about anything, your general understanding of the subject will be significantly more than if you choose a niche and items in which you have no interest and no knowledge. Your product search will be more productive if you start with a firm foundation of interest and expertise. You'll be able to get rid of things quickly that you don't care about or that are of poor quality and won't sell well.

Professional Background

Another technique for finding the best products to sell is to look at things from the perspective of someone who has worked with such products professionally. You may not be enthusiastic about the items, but you do know how they function and what their advantages and disadvantages are. You may have come across the products as a result of your own interactions with them or as a result of your work. The most important thing is that you will be able to confidently answer client questions and provide educated and factual responses. Another benefit of selecting products from a professional standpoint is that you will be aware of market gaps and areas where there is a clear need for products in that industry.

Fads versus Trends

Fads come and go, and what is fashionable today may be obsolete tomorrow. Your goal is to generate money, thus you must first be able to distinguish between fad and trend in order to profit. Fads are non-essential gimmicks that are easily forgotten.

Ask yourself two questions when looking for contemporary things to add to your specialty. Is there a need for this product, and does it solve an issue for users? A trend meets a need or solves a problem, whereas a craze is exciting or entertaining for a few weeks or months before people become bored and move on to something else.

What irritates and irritates people?

Put yourself in the shoes of a buyer when researching your items.

What are the annoyances and disappointments that people have to deal with on a daily basis? The goal is to find products that will make customers' lives easier and those they will undoubtedly want to acquire.

Others' Hobbies and Interests

You don't have to be personally interested in a subject; instead, look into other people's hobbies and interests to see whether there is a market for things relevant to their interests. Searching for hobbies, top hobbies, or popular hobbies is a good place to start.

Going through hobby periodicals, especially those specialised to certain pastimes, is another fantastic source of information. Using social media groups as a research tool is another option. Look at what they're saying, what they're buying, and the lingo they're using. Make a list of words that are peculiar to an activity; they will come in handy when searching.

Learn about people who have unique interests, as everything you learn about your potential customer base may be used to develop marketing tactics for things that they are passionate about.

Availability in your area

You must choose your specialty carefully in order for your dropshipping business to be financially viable. People will easily pop out and pick up your specialty products from their nearby retailer if they are freely available at local retailers. People are impatient, and they will not wait for things to be delivered if they can pick them up on their way home from work.

You have access to global marketplaces, which dramatically expands your supplier base, and you can identify a wonderful niche and goods that customers desire but aren't available in local stores by conducting research.

Check out What Your Competitors Are Doing It's easy to fall into the trap of thinking that if there is little or no competition for the niche you desire, it's excellent and you'll be able to dominate the market. Investigate your competition to understand who you're up against, as there are typically excellent reasons why other companies aren't supplying these things.

The reasons behind this range from a lack of demand for certain products to the fact that there is so little profit to be earned that other companies have moved away from them. It's also possible that the shipping and packing expenses are too high, or that production challenges are too difficult to overcome, making these products unprofitable to invest in.

When deciding on the right niche for you, you must evaluate all of the elements listed above. You may not enjoy having to compete, but competition implies that your items are in high demand, and that your company will be able to survive in the long run with these things.

Chapter Seven: Source And Procure Top-Notch Suppliers

Not all vendors are created equal; some are exceptional or good, while others are mediocre or worse. This is the reality that all new dropshipping businesses confront, and you need to know what to look for in suppliers, how to deal with them, and what to avoid right from the start.

Before you contact suppliers, be sure you're legal.

When you begin sourcing and contacting potential suppliers and wholesalers, you must first set up your business legally and have all of your paperwork in order. This is critical since suppliers will want confirmation of your legality before doing business with you. It's fine to start with basic questions; suppliers are used to entrepreneurs seeking information and will respond without requiring verification of your legal status.

Suppliers and wholesalers will not do business with companies that have not been approved by them, and in order to get that approval, you must be lawfully formed and follow all state regulations. Unfortunately, wholesalers have discovered the hard way that far too many people try to defraud them. So, make sure all of your paperwork is in order, and you'll be on your way to developing positive connections with your suppliers right away.

Suppliers and wholesalers are known for being eccentric and unique, so finding the ones you really want to work with will require some creative thinking. Suppliers do not try to hide from entrepreneurs; they simply march to the beat of their own drum. To get the greatest results, you'll need to conduct some thorough research and follow the suggestions below.

Extensive Searches

Marketing is not a high priority for suppliers when it comes to their products.

To obtain the information you require, you will have to slowly sift through a vast number of search results. When looking for a certain product, the official website of the supplier is usually only located on Page 6 or Page 10 of the search results. You will enjoy the benefits if you persevere.

Make a change to your search criteria.

You must adapt your queries; simply searching for supplier X or product Y will not enough. At best, your search results will be average. Make a list of synonyms, such as wholesaler and supplier, and conduct a search on each of them. To get the greatest search results, use alternate language and different search terms.

Not aesthetically pleasing, yet functional

When you visit a website, you usually look for things that appeal to you, products that capture your eye right away, and websites that keep your attention with snappy online content and high-quality photographs.

Wholesalers and suppliers have basic and effective websites that, to many young entrepreneurs, appear old fashioned and obsolete. They understand that clients require them and will seek them out, so they do not waste time and resources constructing websites to woo potential customers. Learn to look past their websites' external design; it isn't a sign of a terrible provider or mediocre things on offer.

The Benefits of Using Paid Supplier Directories

Using supplier directories is a hotly discussed topic, since some believe it is an unnecessary expense that you won't use again once you've chosen your suppliers. There is no right or incorrect answer; each entrepreneur must make his or her own decision.

These databases are quite useful to have on hand since they are organised and categorised so that you can find all of the suppliers for specific products in one place, and they are routinely updated. Most of the leading firms that provide paid supplier directories test companies before adding them to the directories to ensure that all of their listings are genuinely operating wholesalers and suppliers.

Another advantage of using paid directories is that you will have access to a big number of alternative suppliers for your specialty items in the event of an emergency and the need to switch providers rapidly.

Supplier directories aren't a must-have for your business, but they are a trustworthy and useful tool to have on hand when you need it or want to start scaling up.

A Trick of the Trade to Keep in Your Back Pocket

When you're in a need, you can employ the tried-and-true strategy of making a small order with one of your dropshipping competitors. If you've been unsuccessful in finding a provider, this can be really useful.

Once you've received your order from your competition, you can quickly and easily look up the return address on your item on the internet to find out who initially shipped it to you.

Increase your supplier's trustworthiness.

In the ever-changing world of e-commerce, credibility is a necessary currency for your dropshipping business to succeed. Put yourself in the position of suppliers and wholesalers to see how critical this is. They are continuously dealing with eager business owners who may or may not become their clients. They don't have the time or willingness to deal with people who aren't sure what they want, and they frequently try to use the provider as a free sounding board for inquiries and recommendations.

When approaching a supplier, be decisive and professional. Don't be ambiguous about your business objectives, and don't demand terms and discounts before you've even begun placing orders with them.

Credibility cannot be commanded; it must be gained over time via interactions with the supplier. If you are pushy and demanding when you first start working with a supplier, you will be classified as an unpleasant upstart who should be avoided at all costs, and you will find it difficult to shake that poor reputation.

Pick up the phone and get personal.

Without ever having personal touch with individuals, we live in a world of instant communication via email, chat applications, and social media. Change your thinking when looking for a new provider and create personal contact by picking up the phone. Speak to them, hear their voice, and you'll realise that humans are considerably more approachable than text on a screen.

Suppliers are used to addressing queries from consumers and will accommodate you, which will help you and the supplier develop a positive relationship. Make a list of questions you need answered if he is a new supplier and you are nervous approaching him for the first time.

Set up Test Orders

When you wish to place orders with a new supplier, it's a good idea to test the waters first. Even if you've done extensive research and are confident in the supplier's ability to complete order fulfilment successfully, you should still do so.

For the first few orders, place tiny orders to observe how this particular supplier or wholesaler does his business. This will allow you to monitor how well the company handles the ordering procedure as well as the time it takes to ship goods to your clients. Take note of how promptly the supplier sends you tracking information and how quickly the company's billing department sends you an invoice.

You can ask your consumers for input on the packaging they received and measure their satisfaction with the packaging, shipping, and delivery.

Supplier Qualities to Look for

When choosing your suppliers, be sure they are reputable and trustworthy. You can't leave your business's success in the hands of a supplier who is reckless or has a history of late shipments. Suppliers are critical to any dropshipping business, and you must be confident that the supply is trustworthy. So, while deciding whether or not a particular supplier will be successful in his role, utilise the characteristics listed below as a guide. You should seek for a supplier who possesses the majority, if not all, of the required characteristics.

Members of Staff Who Are Well-Trained and Well-Informed

Competent suppliers with knowledgeable employees who can answer inquiries about the products they sell in a professional manner. If the sales personnel is unable to completely answer inquiries regarding the industry they represent or the various items they sell, it reflects poorly on the supplier's ability to maintain a well-run business. You need a supplier you can trust, especially if you're starting a new firm or expanding into a new niche you don't know much about.

Technology that is up to date

E-commerce in all of its manifestations is strongly reliant on current technology. Check to see if the prospective supplier has kept up with the technologies required to provide a smooth transition from ordering to shipping to delivery.

The supplier's website does not need to be flashy; instead, it should be really functional, so see if he has invested in the following online trade essentials.

Online catalogue with everything.

Data feeds that can be tailored to meet the needs of individual clients.

Real-time inventory that can be accessed.

If you're using suppliers from within the country, you'll need to know where they are.

When using locally sourced supplies, it's important to know where the supplier is located. The more central the supplier's position, the better for your business it is. Local shipping is well-known for taking much longer than shipping into the country from abroad. Your shipment time will be greatly reduced if your supplier is located centrally. Lower shipping prices and happier customers are generally the result of shorter shipping times.

Ordering Method of Preference

Find out how the provider receives orders in different ways. You don't want to be limited to placing all of your orders over the phone. This is inconvenient because you are limited to business hours.

If you're only allowed to place purchases manually through the supplier's website, the process is slow and time-consuming. To free up more time to concentrate on other duties, you'll need to choose the third method of placing orders via email.

Dedicated Support Personnel to Assist You

It can be aggravating to have to deal with a different support staff member each time you phone the supplier. You'll have to repeat yourself several times because the personnel you're dealing with has no idea why you phoned in the first place. When you need to fix a problem, this is extremely inconvenient and time-consuming. A good provider will assign a dedicated support person to deal with your orders and questions.

Avoid Wholesalers and Suppliers

There are various red flags that should alert you to stay away from a particular supplier or wholesaler. Instead, search for a provider who does business honestly and does not coerce clients with deceptive techniques. As soon as you notice any of these symptoms, be cautious and avoid becoming engaged with providers.

Negative Feedback

Examine the supplier's website for negative comments from prior customers, as well as social media, to determine how many complaints there have been. Consumer complaint websites provide a solid indication of a supplier's reviews and comments.

Products in large quantities

As a recommended supplier for your dropshipping business, companies who specialise in the selling of very cheap bulk products do not inspire confidence.

To Be Able to Do Business With Them, They Demand Ongoing Fees

Suppliers who charge you monthly or annual fees for the "luxury" of doing business with them should be avoided at all costs. This is a sort of coercion to which you should never succumb.

Pre-Order Fees That Are Exceptionally High

Pre-order costs are a fact of life for all dropshipping firms, and they vary depending on the sort of order you place, its quantity, and whether it's a bulk purchase or a particularly sophisticated one. What is unusual is a provider who charges considerably greater pre-order fees than is customary; this is not an ethical business practise.

Policy on Non-Negotiable Minimum Size

This supplier is not suited for your dropshipping business if he is unable to be flexible with his minimum order size policy. Many suppliers are willing to charge you a minimum order size fee up front and then fulfil your order amounts when your consumers place orders with you over time.

Before you start working with a provider, be sure you know what to expect

Chapter Eight: Shopify

Dropshipping companies rely on online e-commerce retail platforms as a critical component of their operations. The functioning procedures of e-commerce web platforms are not standardised; each has its own set of advantages and disadvantages. Shopify is one of the most widely used platforms for a variety of reasons.

What exactly is Shopify?

Shopify is an all-in-one e-commerce platform. You construct an online store on the platform for a monthly subscription fee, from which you can market and sell your products globally. Shopify has put together an outstanding set of tools to help you set up your business, including payment gateway integration and support for over 50 languages.

Shopify provides round-the-clock customer service, including 24/7 phone support and live chat to help with any issues that may arise.

For Beginners, the Advantages of Using Shopify in Your Dropshipping Business

For anyone starting out in the dropshipping business, e-commerce platforms can be overwhelming, but Shopify makes it as simple as possible. They provide tools to assist you in setting up your Shopify account, as well as being very dropshipping friendly.

Shopify often posts tutorials and case studies to assist new clients in learning how to use the retail platform. They also share success stories on a regular basis to encourage new entrepreneurs who may be hesitant to start a firm.

Templates & Themes, both free and paid

When you create your Shopify store, you can choose from a wide range of professional themes and templates that are ready to use. The templates are focused on the customer and are mobile-friendly. All of the templates are highly responsive and simple to use. The fact that you are not limited to solely paid for designs and themes is a significant bonus for someone just getting started with dropshipping. The free templates are excellent, and you won't have to spend any money straight away. If you want to have more more features and increased customisation, you can upgrade to paid themes and templates at a later time.

Built-in SEO features

E-commerce in all forms is fiercely competitive and rapidly expanding. To succeed, you'll need all the assistance and support you can obtain. The majority of business owners are not SEO gurus, thus this can be a time-consuming aspect of their operations. Shopify does all of the legwork for you when it comes to SEO by providing all of the tools you'll need to be seen and indexed by search engines. Today, search engine exposure is a must-have for any company.

The following features are accessible to use: adding and updating meta tags, adding product descriptions, and organising products into collections.

Cross-Channel Marketing

The flexibility to sell across several channels is a major benefit to your company.

You can link your Shopify store to a Facebook page and sell directly through the Shopify app, greatly expanding your potential customer base. You can make cross channel sales on other platforms, such as Twitter and Pinterest, using social networking as a marketing strategy. Conduct some research to identify platforms that support cross-channel sales.

An App Store with a Large Selection

Shopify has created a big number of applications to help their customers. These apps increase the possibilities of your Shopify business. These plugins and extensions allow you to choose the ones that best suit your Shopify store's needs. With over 1,500 apps to select from, both paid and free, you can check stock availability and report, provide customer care, and interact with social media much more easily. All of these tools and apps are designed to increase your sales and prospective consumer base while also improving your internet exposure.

Even with the best assistance, problems arise in the workplace, and you may be unsure how to handle them. The Shopify community forum is a terrific way to ask questions, voice issues, and receive advice from Shopify users all over the world.

Language Assistance

This is a significant element of the Shopify platform: it supports all languages. For your store, checkout, and all customer email correspondence, you can choose the language of your choice.

Oberlo Pushes Shopify to New Heights

When Shopify bought the Oberlo app in 2017, it shook up the e-commerce sector, and all Shopify sellers benefited greatly. With Oberlo, you may link to Aliexpress, China's and the Far East's largest online retail platform.

The Oberlo app is only available to Shopify sellers; it does not work with other online retail platforms.

The Most Important Features Oberlo Offers Users Customization

You can make significant modifications to your product descriptions, as well as edit or add photos and product titles.

Filter for ePackets

This filter allows you to select items with the quickest delivery times and import only those items.

Wish Lists You can establish several desire lists for Aliexpress products, and you don't need to switch to import the products from your wish lists — you can do so right from your wish lists.

Dashboard for Sales Monitoring

You can keep track of your costs, revenues, and sales using the sales tracking dashboard.

Accounts for multiple users

This feature gives you freedom because it allows you to delegate management of your online store to others.

It's Possible to Connect Existing Products

You can connect your Aliexpress products to Oberlo if you already sell them.

Pricing is automated.

The ability to define pricing rules so that you can price products in bulk rather than individually.

Tracking of Deliveries

You can keep track of your orders at any moment thanks to the integrated order tracking.

Suppliers should be changed

To take advantage of the greatest costs, you can quickly switch from one supplier to another.

Plans and Pricing

All new clients receive a 30-day free trial of the Pro Plan, which includes all of the app's primary features without the need to input payment card information.

After the trial period has ended, billing will begin.

Starter Strategy

This plan is completely free, but it comes with the following restrictions and features:

Customers purchases are automatically fulfilled. Daily sync of your products. Sales reports. Automatic pricing. You get access to the Oberlo Supply marketplace. The free Oberlo Chrome extension.

Basic Strategy

You can set up 10,000 goods for a fixed monthly charge with the following features and stipulations:

Each month, a maximum of 500 orders will be accepted.

All of the features of the beginner plan are included.

Fulfillment is being monitored.

Shipment tracking is a service that allows you to keep track of your shipments.

Plan for Success

Up to 30,000 goods can be sold.

Orders are not limited.

All of the basic plan's features are included.

Various stores with a large number of users

Advantages of the Oberlo App

Access to Oberlo's broad dropshipping supplier list, which has an established track record.

Aliexpress import is safe, quick, and simple.

To handle products, a high-tech dashboard with a user-friendly interface is used.

Products can be made to order.

Order fulfilment that is automated.

Significant time and labour savings.

Additional scalability.

Users can get help and guidance via video tutorials and the Oberlo blog.

One-click integration with your Shopify store.

Your inventory and prices are automatically updated.

You have access to the Oberlo supplier marketplace and pricing markups.

Tracking of sales and shipments, as well as an ePacket filter.

Although only Aliexpress is supported, Oberlo can be integrated with your Amazon store.

Importing products and managing orders is made easier with this free Google Chrome extension.

Ability to swiftly and conveniently switch product providers.

The Drawbacks of Using Oberlo

Oberlo was created to function exclusively with Shopify. It isn't compatible with other standalone websites or online shopping systems.

Aliexpress is the only marketplace that is supported.

Oberlo does not allow you to update products; instead, you are referred to your Shopify product description page.

Using Shopify Has Its Drawbacks

Shotify has a lot of advantages, but like any other online retail platform, it has some disadvantages that all dropshipping companies should be aware of before deciding to use it.

CMS Restrictions

Your major priority as a dropshipping business is e-commerce sales, and you want to choose a platform that allows you a lot of flexibility while also being simple to use. The Shopify CMS is not comparable to, say, Wordpress, which is a big content management system.

Shopify's content management system is designed for running an e-commerce store, so you'll need to use a bespoke theme with modification possibilities, as well as the Shopify blogging platform, for your dropshipping needs. With adjustments, the SMS constraints can be overcome.

Content restraints

There are just two forms of material to choose from: a page or a blog post. This is troublesome when you want to link posts to specific products and it's difficult to produce additional text fields for any of the products you sell.

Product Lookups

The search features of Shopify's entry-level plans are weak, with no option for complex search filtering. You'll need to upgrade your Shopify plan to get access to the more powerful search capabilities.

Payments

Other than Shopify Payment, Shopify discourages the use of third-party payment processors. If you use one of the other payment gateways, Shopify will charge you a 2% transaction fee for each transaction handled through that gateway.

Expenses

There isn't a single online retail platform that offers their services for free. When you join Shopify, you must review the various costs that they impose in order to make an informed decision about which payment plan you can afford and which will best suit your company needs.

Shopify allows you to check out the platform for free for 14 days so you can have a better understanding of how it works and what your individual business needs are.

To continue utilising the online shopping site after your 14-day trial period, you must choose a subscription plan. They do provide savings for annual and two-year subscription plans, which is a positive. Each payment plan has its own set of benefits, with the higher-priced choices having additional features.

There are five different alternatives available right now:

Basic Shopify. Shopify. Advanced Shopify. Shopify Plus. Shopify Lite. Basic Shopify. Shopify. Advanced Shopify. Shopify Plus (this plan has negotiable fees).

Scalability

Most dropshipping businesses begin small and grow as their resources and money expand. When you reach the point where you want to expand, exporting everything you've done on Shopify is a difficult task because all of the information you've uploaded, as well as any features you've customised, is hosted by Shopify.

The search engine rating you've earned can't be transferred to your new site. Your new site will have to start over, be indexed, and rebuild its search rating from the ground up.

It is not impossible to export data to your new site, but it will require a significant amount of time and effort on your part to export your client and sales data.

The solution to the Shopify scalability issue is to start your dropshipping business with your own website rather than relying entirely on a retail platform. It takes more effort at first, but the long-term advantages are well worth it. Use the platform and gradually construct your website on top of it, so that when you need to scale, you've already built a solid foundation with a CMS that has all the functionality of a big content management system.

Young Entrepreneurs

To open a Shopify account, you must be at least 18 years old. This isn't a major disadvantage; it's merely something that very young entrepreneurs should be aware of. If you are under the age of 18, your parents or guardians must create a Shopify account on your behalf before you can begin.

Chapter Nine: EBAY

Ebay is the e-commerce industry's largest online auction retail platform today's marketplace They cater to the demands of first-time vendors dropshipping, timers, infrequent sellers, big and bulk sellers businesses.

Dropshipping Policies on eBay Dropshipping is legal on eBay as long as the items are in good condition.

He sources his own manufacturers, wholesalers, and dropshippers for his dropshipping business as well as suppliers

You can't list things on eBay that come with a warranty from any other shipping platform, marketplace, or merchant eBay does not allow you to sell things directly to your consumers.

Dropshipping on the basis of arbitrage.

The dropshipping vendor must ensure that his products are delivered on time.

Within 30 days of the listing's publication, a supplier will be found ends.

eBay holds the dropshipping company liable for his actions customer satisfaction with purchased items and timely delivery purchases made during the specified timeframe

If the dropshipping company does not follow eBay's policies, dropshipping will be subjected to penal sanctions a company that consists of the following:

- Listings are being cancelled.

- Listings come to an end for administrative reasons.

- Listings will be removed from search results or degraded.

- It's possible that the seller's rating will be decreased.

- Purchase or sale restrictions may be imposed.

- Protection for the seller or buyer will be withdrawn.

- The dropshipping account has been suspended business.

- All fees, both paid and payable, will be forfeited.

- eBay has taken action against accounts and listings against.

- No action may be taken against your account once it has been taken.

- You will receive a refund or credit for your fees.

How to Succeed at eBay Dropshipping by Working Smart

You must be competitive in order to succeed with dropshipping on eBay.

The profit margins on dropshipping are slim. Your goal is to sell as much as possible.

Although it is conceivable, more selling equals more work for you in terms of listing and processing orders through your provider, and guarantee that each sale is delivered one at a time.

Streamline

Finding products within your eBay search parameters is the greatest approach to streamline your eBay job your chosen niche that you may sell in bulk or as individual listings on eBay variants. As you list these products, this significantly reduces your workload.

It only happens once. If you're not sure how to use these listings, you can look through them all.

In their assistance area, you'll find everything you need to know. You can quickly reduce the size of your document time spent modifying the listing duration and re-listing your products

Availability

A dropshipping business's problem is out of stock and discontinued products nightmare. You can't afford a string of bad evaluations for your company.

Customers who are dissatisfied and who have a large number of complaints do not go unnoticed.

This could put your eBay store in jeopardy. eBay has a lot of rules.

If you receive too many, your account will be terminated customer grievances

It is not difficult to avoid any of this. You must be at the top of your game and receive stock updates from your vendors on a daily basis Check the supply on a regular basis.

Keep track of the things you order from your vendors' movements when the stock market is at its lowest point.

Your reputation as a trustworthy supplier is crucial, and there is simply too much at stake.

There is too much competition in e-commerce for you to overlook this crucial step a part of your company

Customers' Profiles

Many elements influence your eBay success. It's similar to putting together a puzzle.

Each puzzle piece has a specific position and must fit together precisely.

This is where your consumers' demographics come into play.

Create a profile of persons who might be interested in purchasing the item things you have to provide Their age group is particularly significant because it will most likely determine how successful they are.

Their daily habits are most likely to be determined by them. These demographics will provide results.

You'll have a decent notion of what time of day they're most active, as well as which days they're most active.

They're more than likely to shop on eBay. You will be able to change the times as a result of this and the days on which you work on your product listings

It's All About the Timing

The time of day, the day of the week, and the month are all factors is crucial aspects to consider when advertising your products in order to attract the most customers

The goal is to attract as many consumers as possible and close the sale as quickly as feasible.

You can do so and increase your profits.

Peak hours certainly attract the most prospective clients, and for many businesses, these are the busiest times of the day.

This is the way to proceed with dropshipping firms. This is both a plus and a minus.

For a variety of reasons, this is a disadvantage.

Everyone wants to list during peak hours, so you'll have a lot of competition.

There is a lot more competition during peak traffic hours than there is during off-peak traffic hours.

Because of the large number of people who are active on eBay around this time. During certain hours, you may notice that the site is significantly slower than usual.

This is not uncommon, and it can be a major issue at the time of an auction closes. People scurry from eBay store to eBay store in search of the best deals and products, and if your website is slow, you may lose business.

Customers may not be able to access your ads in time for the auction to begin and ends.

Your consumer demographics will tremendously assist you in avoiding overwhelming situations.

If you've done your homework, you'll be able to count on a large number of competitors and a rush at peak hours.

Do some demographic research to find out when your consumers are most likely to buy.

Take a look at eBay.

You must balance the prospective income during peak times for optimal success hours, as well as the timetables of your target audience. It all depends on the situation whether your niche products are niche, and whether your target demographic is average shopper group that will be out shopping at the same time as almost everyone else shopping, or if they'd rather do their online buying at another time purchases.

Customer Service

The consumer is at the centre of any business, and your goal for your firm is to please them.

The goal of a dropshipping business is to not only attract but also retain consumers.

Return to place further orders. It cannot be overstated how important

It is critical to cultivate positive relationships with your consumers.

Gaining a reputation for dependability is crucial to developing great relationships.

Customers must be able to trust that they will be able to obtain the things that you offer you've listed, and that you'll make sure customers get their packages as soon as possible.

It will be in perfect shape when it arrives.

Your customers must know that you will stand behind them if an issue arises.

They will go to great lengths to ensure that you find solutions and that you are successful.

They will be pleased with the outcome. No matter how difficult a situation is, there is always a solution.

You cannot afford to be abrupt with clients in this situation even when they are acting irrationally and yelling empty threats aimed towards you

Price Stabilization

People want to get the best deal on whatever they're buying, and will scour the market for the best deals. It's possible that this will be a logistical nightmare.

Because dropshipping businesses must deal with a variety of expenses,

Costs of subscriptions and rates levied by your suppliers being able to

You can make a profit, keep your customers happy, and operate your business efficiently if you follow these steps.

You should be aware of how these four key factors influence your prices variables:

- Supplier prices are set in stone.
- Final sales prices are subject to change.

eBay charges two types of fees: listing fees and percentages of the final transaction price.

You must be able to successfully regulate prices while yet making the most profit possible should put the following methods into action and make the most of your possibilities advantage.

Use the Buy It Now option in the listing. You sell the products you've posted.

The advantage of a fixed price is that you can then make the profit you want a goal for

Buy it Now charges a one-time insertion fee that is applied to multiple items in addition to individual listings The insertion fee is usually fixed.

Fees are lower than those charged by other listing services.

Another way to exert control over a listing is to place a reserve price on it pricing. The reserve price is the lowest amount you will accept as a bid customers' feedback on that specific auction item

When using the reserve price option, be careful not to overpay.

Don't forget to adjust your reserve price to account for this.

Fees for final value and insertion vary. The disadvantage of using

The disadvantage of reserved pricing is that your customers are unable to see what the reserve is.

It's all about price, and this can be very irritating for your customers.

eBay provides a free calculator to help you figure out your costs.

Various eBay fees may apply. This is a very useful tool for saving money time and lessen stress when having to calculate all the fees and costs involved with trading on eBay.

- To have more control over your profit margin, you can opt for setting a higher starting bid in order for you to cover the fixed costs that you have no control over. These include your eBay listing fees and final value fees, as well as supplier costs and all applicable taxes and shipping costs.

Product Fulfillment

Keeping track of the whole fulfilment process is critical as you are competing with countless sellers daily on eBay. If your customers are unhappy, they will very quickly go and find what they are looking for from another seller and your reputation will soon be in shreds.

The fulfilment process can be frustrating for any dropshipping business as you do not physically handle the products, you fully rely on your suppliers to accomplish fulfilment smoothly and fast.

You want to source and retain suppliers that have their finger on the pulse of their business and will keep you up to date during the fulfilment process and immediately contact you to inform you should there be a problem or the possibility of delays. This will allow you to communicate with your customer before a situation gets out of hand.

Advantages of eBay Dropshipping Ease of Use

Anyone with basic computer abilities may easily negotiate on eBay. It's designed to help you set up your store in the shortest amount of time possible and to make running your store as simple as possible. You can use a variety of plugins and tools to help you.

Visibility

eBay is a hugely popular online auction site with a never-ending stream of visitors wanting to buy anything under the sun. This increases the visibility of your eBay dropshipping business, allowing you to reach as many potential buyers as possible in your sector.

Effort: Working Smarter, Not Harder

You have the opportunity to make sales with less work and at the best possible pricing because of the large number of daily visitors who can read your listings on eBay.

No technical knowledge is required.

Setting up and running an eBay store does not necessitate any technological knowledge. Everything is in place for you; all you have to do now is focus on product sourcing and listing.

Marketing

Because your company has such a huge audience, you won't have to spend as much money on marketing or investing in sponsored traffic and SEO. This is critical, particularly if you are new to the dropshipping business concept.

System for Detecting Fraud

The eBay rating system is beneficial to both the vendor and the buyer. After each sale, both the consumer and the seller are given the chance to rate their experience, give a favourable, neutral, or negative rating, and leave a comment about the specific sale, which aids in fraud protection.

When customers post unusually bad reviews, the evaluation system helps to warn you as the seller. You then have the choice to accept or reject the transaction, as well as to explain why the sale was declined. Please keep in mind that this only applies to unusual cases. Under normal circumstances, the seller is not permitted to make critical remarks; the only options available to the seller are praise and a review.

PayPal

eBay has integrated Paypal, allowing you to take real-time payments while also providing much-needed protection to the seller.

Ratings

Your eBay credit rating informs potential consumers about your creditworthiness. All sellers on eBay are rated on three levels. The ratings are determined on the level of service you provide as well as your sales history. Each month, the evaluation ratings are completed, and in e-commerce, the rating system can either bring more customers or have a negative impact on your business if your rating is very low.

Best Sellers

This grade informs all potential consumers that you've met the minimum sales requirement for this category. This rating also qualifies you for Top Rated Plus listing privileges, provided you meet the listing requirements.

Above Average

You've satisfied the eBay minimal requirements for all sellers, and your customer service is satisfactory.

Below Average

You have failed to meet one or more of eBay's customer service basic criteria. If your rating is below par, eBay may take action against you by moving your listings to the bottom of the eBay search results.

Dropshipping Fees on eBay Have Drawbacks

When you have an eBay store, you must pay a variety of fees.

When you sell through an online platform, you pay fees that you wouldn't have to pay if you just sold your things through your own website. Due to increased competition, the profit margin on online platforms is reduced, making listing fees an additional expense. If you offer things with optional extras, the fees will increase with each additional option you select.

Customization

You don't have any options for personalising your store in order to make it distinctive to customers. There are no opportunities to create consumer loyalty through specialised product or niche marketing or inventive sales approaches because everything is standardised.

Competition in a Specific Field

Should your chosen niche products become successful, you may face stiff competition from other eBay sellers selling the same niche products, potentially resulting in a price war.

Payments from Customers

Non-payment by clients is a recurrent issue on eBay, as are issues throughout the checkout process.

Monitoring

If you want to set up a dropshipping store on eBay, you'll need to keep an eye on your listings on a frequent basis if you want to sell enough products.

There are various tools available to aid you in monitoring your listings to make this task easier.

Unfair Criticisms

Customers aren't always pleasant, and disgruntled customers frequently leave venomous, unjustified negative reviews. This is a problem for any firm, but eBay does not remove reviews, regardless of how unfair or out of context they are in relation to the issues that have arisen. Only in extraordinary circumstances will they remove a review. This leaves a permanent record on your account, and if you leave too many nasty reviews, you risk having your account revoked a tenth chapter

AMAZON

mazon is the world's largest online retail platform. Amazon and what they do are well-known. When you set up your dropshipping store and become a member of the Amazon brand, you automatically become affiliated with the Amazon brand. This alone provides significant benefits for your dropshipping business, even before considering all of the other advantages that dropshipping on Amazon provides.

Using the Amazon retail platform for your dropshipping business may be done in a variety of ways, which we'll go over in depth and explain how each type of dropshipping works.

You can use Amazon FBA for dropshipping, and since the products are sent from an Amazon warehouse, Amazon effectively becomes your dropshipper. You may also work with other third-party vendors, but you must follow Amazon's dropshipping policy at all times.

Punitive measures will be taken if you do not follow the policy regulations.

You must be the seller of record for all products you sell on Amazon at all times.

On all packing slips and waybills, as well as any other material provided about the product or included with the product, you must identify yourself as the seller of the products. You are responsible for accepting and processing all products returned by your customers.

All other Amazon policies and the selling agreement must be followed at all times.

You may not purchase products from any other online shop and have them deliver directly to your consumers, and you may not send out any information on invoices, shipping orders, or packing slips other than your own. All information about the seller, such as the seller's name and contact information, must be yours and not that of another company.

If you do not follow this dropshipping policy to the letter, your account will be suspended and all of your selling privileges will be withdrawn.

Tools for Dropshipping

There are a plethora of dropshipping tools that work with the Amazon platform. This can be perplexing for companies who are just starting out in the dropshipping business. You can investigate the different tools available as you gain experience. The tools listed below are the ones you'll need right away to help you expand your dropshipping business and make it worthwhile to invest in.

Express Your Opinion

You need as much good feedback from clients as possible to drive sales and develop your dropshipping business. Positive feedback is boosted and bad feedback is removed with the help of Feedback Express. This is the most effective strategy to keep your store and the products you offer in good standing.

Another feature of Feedback Express is that it allows you to ban consumers who have left unjustified negative reviews.

The Buy Box is a tremendous boost to sales for all Amazon sellers, and the variables used to determine who wins the Buy Box are your feedback score and your seller rating.

This tool also provides you notifications on your phone anytime a negative review of your service or products is left on your store.

This tool comes with personalised email templates with an auto insert function for images, logos, links, and order information to make things even easier for you.

You have a 30-day free trial with FeedBack Express when you first sign up, with the option to purchase at the end of your trial term.

FeedCheck FeedCheck collects all of your product reviews in one location so you can see them all at once. If you have numerous listings, this is a useful tool to utilise because it allows you to check how each one is performing and informs you when you need to improve your customer service to improve your ratings. This application can also be used to keep track of your competitors' items.

You can choose from three different package options.

Initiation. This is for the new Amazon reseller who is just getting started. This package includes a seven-day free trial period.

Developing a Brand This is the greatest option for a company that sells a small number of products that are accessible from a variety of other merchants. You have a seven-day free trial period with the option to purchase.

Entrepreneurship. This is a better alternative for consumer products companies, agencies, and big brands. This bundle includes customised pricing based on the quantity of products, infinite store channels, and client-specific requirements.

Merchant Phrases

The Merchant Words app gathers information about the words and phrases Amazon users use to search for products via the Amazon autocomplete search bar. High-ranking keywords and product trends are identified using the data.

There are three subscription levels to choose from: silver, gold, and platinum.

Amazon regional, per country, and global data, as well as monthly searches, are included in the app.

Keyword seasonality, keyword collections, keyword search volumes, and Pge One analysis.

ASIN plus is a service that allows you to find out more about a product.

Multiple users. Keyword history.

Keyword multiplier, performance analytics, and a digital shelf dashboard.

Tools for Amazon Volume Listings

Amazon has created a number of tools to help you manage inventory and purchase information more effectively, including printable spreadsheets. Product quantities and pricing can be changed and modified rapidly using listing tools.

Sellery is an Amazon repricing solution that adapts to marketing conditions in real time, employing a vast number of price combinations to create a unique pricing plan for your Amazon store. Continuous monitoring is accomplished by sophisticated filters that react quickly to changes in order to keep you competitive.

Pricing begins at 1% of your monthly sales, with a minimum charge of $50 and a maximum price of $150 each month. A 14-day trial period is included with the product.

Scheduled repricing is one of the features.

Real-time repricing and pricing regulations that are automatically applied.

Private labelling solutions are available.

Pricing solutions that can be tailored to meet the demands of individual clients.

All of the features increase your chances of winning the coveted Buy Box, including net margin management and Amazon professional support.

Shopify

In 2017, Shopify announced a partnership with Amazon. This means you can now integrate your Amazon store as a sales channel to your Shopify store. It only takes a few minutes to connect your Shopify products with your Amazon listings. If you have Amazon sales that need to be fulfilled, Shopify will notify you. This connection provides you with a plethora of additional sales opportunities to help you expand your dropshipping business.

Incorporate a Product Tool

Rather of using bulk listing, this interactive tool is used to add each product one at a time to modest quantities of products. The following tasks are suited for this web-based interface:

To establish a new listing on Amazon for a product that does not yet exist. When you add a new product to Amazon that isn't currently for sale, they build a product description page for it.

To match a product listing that already exists. You must match the product you wish to sell to the product detail page that already exists.

Approvals and Restrictions on Products

Before you start selling on Amazon, you'll need to figure out which category your products belong in. It is critical that you read the limited products help pages on the Amazon official website. The standards controlling all products offered for sale on Amazon's online retail platform are extremely rigorous.

Before you establish your Amazon store or add new products to your store, you must first determine which category the products come into and what standards and laws you must follow.

Failure to follow these regulations can result in your account being deleted and you being barred from using Amazon in the future.

Amazon's items are divided into three categories.

Restricted products that require clearance, with some products requiring state or country-specific approval as well as approval according to Amazon's own regulations.

Prohibited products are those that are not allowed to be listed on Amazon at all.

As the seller, it is your responsibility to ensure that all of your listings are in order and that the effort spent doing so is well worth it. You put in a lot of effort to start your dropshipping business, and you deserve to reap the rewards. There's no reason for your business to fail because of rules and restrictions.

Fees Paid by the Seller

Fees are a disadvantage that all sellers suffer, regardless of the online retail platform they choose. Knowing exactly what seller fees you'll be dealing with and how they differ between selling plans can help you determine which selling plan is ideal for your company and will have the least impact on your profit.

Please keep in mind that all of the fees listed below apply only to sales in the United States. If you plan to run your dropshipping business out of another country, you'll need to check what fees are relevant in that country.

The professional seller plan and the individual seller plan are also available, with different rates for each.

Fees per item

This fee is charged for each item you sell on Amazon. If you utilise the professional seller plan, you will not be charged a per-item cost.

When you sell something on Amazon, you get paid the whole amount the purchaser paid. This includes delivery charges, per-item charges, any add-ons such as gift wrapping, and any other charges the buyer requested.

Referral Fees Every item sold is subject to a referral charge. A minimum referral fee per item is set for some product categories. When you sell a product that fits inside the minimum referral fee category, you are responsible for either the referral charge or the per-item fee, whichever is greater.

Fees for Shipping

Professional sellers are responsible for shipping fees on media products when orders are not fulfilled by Amazon. On all products sold, individual sellers are responsible for delivery costs. The shipping fees are computed based on the item's category and the expenses associated with that category, as well as the charge for the shipping service selected by the customer. As the seller, you are responsible for these delivery costs.

You will be charged FBA fees when you use the Amazon FBA system, which include storage, fulfilment, and optional additional services. This shipping price is in addition to the fees that must be paid when selling on Amazon.

Closing Fees That Vary

For both professional and individual vendors, this fee is applied to all media items. The fee is calculated based on fees that have been set in advance for each category.

A monthly subscription cost for the Professional Seller Plan.

On every item sold, there is a referral fee that varies by category.

Category-specific variable closure fees; the Amazon marketplace per-item fee is not applicable on this seller plan; shipping fees only apply to media products (DVDs, videos, video games, software, music, and books).

Prepare to sell more than 40 products per month.

Plan for Individual Sellers

This plan does not require a monthly subscription charge.

Each item sold is subject to a per-item cost.

Fees for referrals.

Closing costs are subject to change.

All things sold are subject to shipping charges.

This strategy is for monthly sales of less than 40 products.

Amazon Fulfillment Service is a service provided by Amazon.

Amazon introduced the FBA (Fulfilled by Amazon) dropshipping concept in 2006. The FBA model can be used in a variety of ways.

As the seller, you ship your bulk purchases (minimum size orders from suppliers) to an Amazon warehouse, where they are held and sent to individual consumers as they place orders, with Amazon handling the packaging and shipping.

Dropshipping companies also use Amazon's FBA service to fulfil orders for products sold in their Amazon shop.

You can also utilise the FBA service to fulfil orders that you sell on other online retail platforms, as well as products that you sell directly on your own website. Under the Amazon fulfilment umbrella, you integrate your fulfilment from all of your different stores.

Amazon FBA shifts the goalposts for the dropshipping business model, as it no longer allows you to ship straight from your supplier to your consumer. Even if it's just the minimum order size set by your supplier, you'll need to buy some inventory that will be held in an Amazon warehouse.

FBA Advantages Reliable and Quick Processing

Amazon is the world's largest retail platform, and it has a proven track record of getting products to their destinations as quickly as possible, in pristine condition, and with no mistakes.

Increased Margin

When you buy things to store at Amazon, your suppliers will usually offer you wholesale prices, which is a savings above the prices they provide you when you place individual purchases with them.

Amazon FBA-Specific Advantages

Amazon provides incentives to encourage you to list your products for dropshipping straight on Amazon.

Your conversion rate may increase if you are eligible for the following features:

Super Saver Shipping, Amazon Prime, and Buy Box are all options. Amazon takes care of product returns for you by connecting directly with customers and mailing a replacement item on your behalf.

Storage Fees are a disadvantage.

You must pay to have your inventory stored at an Amazon warehouse.

Because it is not cost-effective to store products with lesser demand, dropshipping businesses normally only store their best-selling products for use with FBA.

Because the products remain their property until you place an order, your suppliers do not charge you for storage.

Fees for using the FBA service are charged, and this reduces your profit margin.

Fees for Long-Term Storage

On things that have been in storage for more than a year, you are responsible for the long-term storage fees. This price is in addition to the regular storage fees that must be paid.

The long-term storage fee is determined per cubic foot and per unit, and the appropriate long-term storage fee is the higher of these two measurement costs.

There isn't any dedicated storage.

Your inventory stored in the warehouse does not have its own storage space. At Amazon, products from all suppliers are grouped into categories, so your inventory will be stored alongside similar products from several providers. When it comes to transporting the product to your client, it could be from any provider, not just your supplier.

You might have an SKU-level sticker put to your individual things to prevent them from being mixed up with the identical product from elsewhere, which costs $0.02 per item to be labelled. This may appear to be an unnecessary expense, but it ensures that your consumer receives the same thing you purchased from your supplier, rather than an item with the same name but worse quality than your original buy.

The Advantages of Amazon Dropshipping

You obtain direct access to the greatest online retail platform's buying audience, both locally and abroad.

The Fulfillment by Amazon system, which includes all of the benefits described in the section titled Amazon Fulfillment Service; Amazon adverts, which allow you to manage how much you spend because Amazon does not require a minimum quantity to use their ads.

You'll spend less money on overhead to run your business.

Order processing, shipping, and marketing automation are all available, as are tools for repricing products, which eliminates the need to update manually.

Buy Box if you have received outstanding reviews.

Dropshipping on Amazon Has Its Drawbacks

Fees for listing.

Extra warehouse storing fees for long-term storage if products are stored for more than 365 days if you use Amazon FBA.

Vulnerability of your sales data because Amazon has access to all of your store's data. This contains your overall sales totals as well as which of your items are the best-sellers.

Because Amazon controls all areas of your marketing and branding, customization is limited.

The dropshipping policy establishes very rigorous guidelines for what a dropshipping company may and may not do.

Punitive measures will be used if you fail to follow any of their policies.

Chapter Ten: Creating Your Own Dropshipping Website

With all of the online retail platforms to select from, as well as the apps and plugins that everyone has access to, the dropshipping business model is highly adaptable. This makes it simple to get started with your dropshipping business. Because of the numerous advantages that come with selling on retail platforms, such as templates, specialised apps, and marketing, many new businesses are content to sell exclusively on these platforms. It's simple and straightforward, and it pays off. This is fantastic, and all dropshipping businesses should take advantage of the various online shopping venues available.

What Is the Importance of Having a Website?

The majority of people ask this question because it appears to be a lot of work for very little reward. There are a number of reasons why you should start constructing your own business website while using online retail platforms.

Your own website establishes credibility for your company in the eyes of potential customers, suppliers, and distributors. It shifts the perception of you as a platform listing or a disembodied store among the thousands of other online stores available on retail platforms.

Manufacturers and suppliers prefer to collaborate with dropshipping companies who already have a website. Even if you're just getting started and have a modest customer base, it shows your suppliers that you're serious about running a business and aren't simply another fly-by-night dropshipping operation looking to make a quick cash and move on. When approaching new suppliers, they will check online to see if you have a website; your website will help you create trust and rapport with them.

Another compelling reason to create your own website is to stay ahead of the competition. Dropshipping businesses with a desire to be seen and successful have their own e-commerce websites. Competitor analysis is one of the most important e-commerce analytics, and not having your own website might hurt your business's success.

Setting the wheels in motion

Not everyone is tech-savvy, and building your own website isn't something everyone is eager to do. You'll need an e-commerce dropshipping-specific website design with as many features as possible to make running your website as simple as possible and to let clients to traverse your website without stumbling blocks caused by poor website design.

You have the option of having a professional create your website based on your exact requirements. You can conduct an internet search to locate the appropriate templates and designs. There are a plethora of decent website creation templates to pick from that will suit your specialty and include all of the functionality you require for your own website.

The cost of setting up your website is determined by your budget, but most of the templates offered are free. These free templates are more basic, but they'll suffice if you're on a budget.

To begin, you'll need to set up your website hosting, with WordPress hosting being the most popular choice among dropshipping extension and plugin users. Select design templates and a domain name that is appropriate.

Hosting a website

The necessity of selecting the best and most cost-effective web hosting solution for your dropshipping business website cannot be overstated. When you're just starting out, having to remember what form of hosting is ideal and what to look for in a web hosting solution can be very confusing. People frequently throw up their hands and choose the first web hosting company they come across while conducting a search in order to avoid having to think about this element. Some of the factors to verify may appear technical, but they are all manageable with the right tools and some effort. To help you make the best decision possible, we've highlighted the most crucial aspects to look for when selecting a web hosting provider.

Reviews

To begin, conduct some research on the web hosting providers you're considering.

Unfortunately, many websites that promise to post reliable reviews leave you down, as web hosting providers dislike bad reviews about their businesses and will go to any length to erase these ratings from the sites where they appear. If you do a Google search for the name of the firm you're looking for and the term reviews, you'll obtain quick and accurate results from websites that publish unpaid reviews.

Reviews

To begin, conduct some research on the web hosting providers you're considering.

Unfortunately, many websites that promise to post reliable reviews leave you down, as web hosting providers dislike bad reviews about their businesses and will go to any length to erase these ratings from the sites where they appear. If you do a Google search for the name of the firm you're looking for plus the term reviews, you'll obtain quick and accurate results from websites that post unpaid evaluations and information from people who have used the specific hosting service's personal blogs.

Limits on Bandwidth and Storage

Because you'll be offering products from many suppliers, you'll need enough storage space to run your dropshipping business. Your hosting service should be able to handle the upload of at least 10,000 goods without difficulty.

Because bandwidth is so vital, make sure you find out whether the hosting provider has bandwidth limits or if it is unrestricted. Customers will download information as they explore your store, and if your hosting service has limitations, this may cause issues, and customers will grow frustrated if they are unable to download information and photos.

Support for PHP 7 and SSL Certificates

The presence or absence of SSL certificates on a website is one of the search engine ranking variables. SSL-enabled websites receive a higher ranking.

Customers get a Google window warning that a website does not have an SSL certificate when they browse. This alerts the user, and the majority of them will leave that site and go to one that they believe they can trust.

Ensure that the web hosting service you select supports PHP 7, the most recent version of PHP. This is especially crucial for your dropshipping website, as some of the most popular dropshipping plugins no longer support older PHP versions.

Pricing

Web hosting services can be prohibitively expensive, especially for an ecommerce firm. Cloud hosting has a lot of cost-cutting benefits like limitless bandwidth and automatic scaling that adjusts when your website gets a lot of traffic.

Performance

The performance of a hosting service can be assessed using the tools provided to determine how fast or slow loading times are, as well as the actual page speed. Another method is to visit websites that use a specific hosting service and see how long they take to load. This will assist you in removing hosting services that perform poorly.

Security

The bulk of today's hosting solutions include cPanel website management. Examine whether the hosting service employs cPanel or another less well-known control panel. You'll need a safe control panel that prevents all back-door access while also allowing secure access via SSH and FTP.

Support for E-Commerce Platforms

Your hosting service should be able to install the most popular e-commerce platforms with a single click.

Service to Customers

A dependable hosting business will provide phone and online help 24 hours a day, seven days a week. Prospective clients must be able to visit your website at any time with minimal service interruptions for your business to succeed.

Ability to Scale

If the hosting service you're considering doesn't offer automatic scaling, you should either look for one that does or double-check that their servers can scale to meet your needs. Your company cannot afford to lose consumers or reduce order placement due to the servers' failure to keep up.

Your Own Web Address

Your domain name is your one-of-a-kind address. Although all computers on the internet have a numeric IP address, people will never recall a single IP address among the billions on the internet. When it was determined that having an IP address was insufficient for finding individual websites, domain names were formed. As a result, your one-of-a-kind address is created by combining a unique IP address with a unique domain name. No company can afford to vanish into online; if customers can't locate you, they'll look for another company that does what you do.

Having your own domain name provides more than just a way for search engines to reach your website; it also has other advantages that many people overlook.

Mobility on the Internet

After you've created your own domain name, it's yours to keep. If you decide to change web hosts or servers, you can keep your domain name. You'll have a lot of troubles if you don't own your domain name. You'll have to start over with a new URL, and you'll lose all of the work you've put into developing your brand.

Credibility

If you don't have a domain name, the web host or ISP will assign you a generic. This is plainly visible on your website address and indicates that your company is not very professional or trustworthy. Humans are not the most trusting creatures, and e-commerce has taken over the world. It is your responsibility to provide them with reasons to trust you and want to conduct business with you. Having a free generic URL communicates to others that you are unwilling to invest in your online presence by acquiring a domain name.

No small business can afford to be characterised as cheap; potential clients will seek out other businesses that demonstrate that they are serious about their work.

It Demonstrates Your Initiative

Your domain name demonstrates that you are keeping up with technological advancements. You don't want to lose a large chunk of your potential consumer base by saving money by employing generic URLs because the younger generations are very tech-savvy and pick up on the finer details.

Select a Domain Name That Is Appropriate

You do not have to choose a domain name that is the same as your business name.

If you choose a domain name that reflects what your business is all about, a phrase that connects online searchers to your niche, it will attract visitors looking for anything related to your topic.

E-Commerce Website Requirements

You want your website to reflect your products and your niche, as well as provide your clients with a memorable shopping experience that will encourage them to return.

Product, design, and content must all be in sync.

You want your clients to link your website to the things you sell and that they want. Every element of your website, including colours, text, photographs, videos, and music, must be tailored to your specialty. Your client demographics are also important; your website should appeal to the type of individual who would be interested in the things you provide.

Shopping Cart with a User-Friendly Interface

Nothing irritates a customer more than becoming bogged down by an online shopping cart that makes it impossible to add, update, or remove things once they've opted to start shopping. When they wish to return and peruse some more, they get stuck and are unable to do so. Because the consumer is king, take your time and examine all of the elements that will make the transaction simple and stress-free.

Keep the check-out process as simple as possible.

Your goal is to make it as simple as possible for your customers to complete the checkout process, since you require the maximum potential sales conversion. Customers quit their shopping cart for a variety of reasons before completing the transaction.

A small percentage of shoppers abandon the check-out procedure because they were merely looking around and comparing costs. You have no say in the matter. Baymard.com examined and analysed what you can influence, and the percentages of carts abandoned for each cause are eye-opening, pointing up methods to make your website more customer-friendly and enticing.

Customers expect their buying to be simple and painless. Your check-out procedure should be simple, quick, and suit the needs of your customers.

n.d. (Baymard Institute)

The Internet and Social Media

Social media has become an important aspect of millions of people's lives.

Making social media a part of your website is critical in today's corporate world. People nowadays use social media to keep up with current events and to see what's being said about a product they might be interested in. Using social media as a marketing strategy draws a big number of people to your items, resulting in a significantly greater conversion rate in sales.

Security

For your dropshipping business, your e-commerce website must have top security features. The Payment Card Industry Data Security Standard (PCI DSS) is a data security standard that must be followed by any website that accepts credit cards.

Shoppers value security so much that it's frequently the first thing they look for on a website, and if it's not secure, they'll leave, no matter how much they want to buy a specific product.

Including the necessary security measures in your website design serves as an incentive for shoppers to become frequent buyers of your products via your website.

Support for several languages

Many business owners are unaware of the significant advantages that including multi-language support into their website may provide. This isn't simply a customer-friendly feature; it also provides you a leg up on competitors that don't offer multi-language support.

Multinational organisations have embraced multilingual help, while smaller e-commerce businesses have mostly ignored it. Smaller businesses can get an early start and reap the rewards while their competitors fall farther behind because e-commerce has become such a large element of all worldwide purchases.

This is an extremely effective marketing technique for expanding your business into international markets and attracting new customers interested in your niche products. Being able to converse in their own tongue will immediately attract their attention. When you include the top world languages, you broaden your potential client base and increase your sales potential by a factor of two.

A multilingual website breaks down cultural barriers and earns international buyers' trust. People are often hesitant to make purchases over the internet in a language they do not fully comprehend.

The majority of the major search engines can conduct searches in languages other than English. With language support, you instantly increase the likelihood of your website being found when consumers search for your products.

Plugins are a must-have.

Plugins are essential for running a dropshipping website. You need them to do the numerous chores that would otherwise suck up your time if you had to do them manually.

The plugins you'll need are dependent on the online retail platform you've partnered with, as some are platform-specific and won't perform effectively on others.

The goal of this article is to introduce you to the plugins that have received the best user evaluations and have received the highest ratings. These are worth trying out on a trial basis to see which ones best suit your website and products.

Dropshipping App Oberlo

This app is best suited for Shopify and can be found in the Shopify app store.

It provides a lot of cool features, like a directory of approved dropship providers, which makes finding new dropship suppliers a breeze. This app is used to sync your Amazon sales channel on Shopify since Amazon integrated with Shopify. There is a free version of the software as well as two paid versions. Please consult Chapter 8, subparagraph 1 for a complete list of Oberlo's features. Oberlo Pushes Shopify to Its Limits.

Rabbit with a Social Life

This WooCommerce software is a social media marketing tool that promotes your website and business automatically.

SEO Plugin This plugin may be found in the Shopify app store. There is a free version as well as a paid version accessible. When there are any concerns with how your website performs on search engines, the free version of Plugin SEO will notify you. It also teaches you how to use basic SEO methods.

AliDropship

The Aliexpress dropshipping plugin for WordPress is provided by AliDropship, which is a premium plugin. This is a plugin for Aliexpress users who want to import products from their website. Because the bulk of features are automated, this plugin is extremely popular.

Alidropship This is the Alidropship WooCommerce plugin, which is a premium plugin that works with WooCommerce. This version of the plugin is more complex than the general original version because it has a modern design and additional functions, making it a superior option a happy egg

This tough plugin is made for WordPress and is really popular among users.

Its purpose is to keep your product information up to date.

Product Evaluations

This WordPress plugin is for product reviews and comes with all of the typical functionality you'll need to review your products.

Dropshix

There are two versions of this plugin. The basic option is free, while the advanced features option costs money. Dropshix keeps track of shipments and generates real-time data that are auto-synchronized. It comes with a Chrome extension built in.

MailChimp

MailChimp is an email marketing plugin that helps you with your business's email marketing. All e-commerce enterprises can use this service to send out mass emails to customers informing them of new products available.

Options for Integration

It provides social media integration options, such as Facebook, as well as access testing and scheduling to improve your open rates. Your marketing will benefit from having no restrictions on picture hosting at free cost.

Templates

MailChimp has a number of basic themes, but you may also import your own. You may also alter the standard templates with a simple point-and-click editor without needing to know how to code.

This plugin is available for free for up to 2,000 contacts. Your subscription form and campaign both feature their logo. The enhanced version of the plugin allows you to remove their logo from all of your company's outgoing mail.

Metrics for Comparison

You can keep track of your email campaigns and analyse how well they're functioning. Another useful feature is the ability to compare your metrics to those of other Mailchimp subscribers.

There is no such thing as a perfect software, plugin, or extension because it is impossible to create them to meet the demands of each individual user. Most functions are sufficiently addressed by MailChimp, but there are a few limitations to be aware of before using this plugin.

Subscription-based and membership-based websites

The MailChimp plugin for WordPress, as well as PayPal, can be difficult at times. You will have problems if your website offers membership and subscription choices. You may also set up autoresponders, but this has the downside of only working with those who have subscribed using one of your online forms and does not work with any contacts you have imported.

The Templates Are Simple and Standard

The templates are uninspiring and unappealing to the readers. To make the MailChimp templates more appealing, you can either spend time altering them or import your own templates that are tailored to your customers' demographics and products.

Problems with the User Interface

The MailChimp interface takes some time to become comfortable with, and some users find it difficult to use. This plugin is ideal for a company that sends out information updates and newsletters, but it might be time consuming if your email volume is huge.

Another disadvantage of the interface is that you cannot send out numerous email lists at the same time. You can only send out subscriber lists one at a time.

Suspension of Accounts is a legal term that refers to the suspension of a

If you receive spam complaints about your emails or a large number of unsubscribe requests, MailChimp retains the right to cancel or suspend your account without warning. To avoid suspension or cancellation, users must be alert and test emails before sending them to their subscribers.

Benefits of Having Your Own Website Reputable Image

Customers will encounter a website that has been built to be professional and customer-focused when they visit your website. People are more likely to spend money with a company that has a professional website rather than a listing on a completely anonymous retail platform.

There will be no competition.

When you have to compete with so many other listings that sell the same or very similar things, it can be a pain. Visitors to your website will only see things that you sell displayed. Prices are frequently driven down to the point where there is no profit margin left on online auction platforms because there are simply too many sellers competing. When selling on your own website, you can set reasonable rates that allow you to make a profit.

Fees for listing and selling homes are decreasing.

If you offer PayPal and similar payment alternatives on your website, you may still have to pay fees depending on the payment options you have.

Many other fees associated with using online retail platforms, such as fees for each product you list, subscription fees, and more, are eliminated.

Disadvantages

Costs of Starting a Business

When you create your own website, you will incur upfront fees, which you should factor into your budget. The first financial investment, however, is determined by the website you choose. Your start-up fees will be significant if you desire a custom-built website designed by a web design company. When you choose to put in some effort, a WordPress website can help you save a lot of money by providing you with a fully functional website with all of the needs.

Support

You do not have access to the support staff that you would get if you subscribed to one of the online shopping platforms. You will be responsible for resolving any issues that arise on your website. If you choose a trustworthy website builder, however, you will have access to their technical support team for help.

Slowly, traffic builds up.

It will take time to create organic traffic when you first establish your own website. You'll have to gradually build up your client base and devoted customers who will return to your website over time.

Chapter Eleven: Your Online Presence

The significance of having a good internet presence cannot be overstated. A company that does not have an online presence simply does not exist on the Internet. No matter how good the things you sell are, the search engines can't locate you. When consumers search for your products and niche, the bigger your online presence is, the easier it is for search engines to locate you.

We'll go through each of the methods you should employ to get the best possible online presence, as well as how each one improves your visibility to search engines and potential clients.

Marketing

An intricately built spider web can be compared to marketing. Every part of your organisation is involved, and it all has to work together to improve your internet presence, expand your customer base, and increase your profit margin.

Many components and types of marketing are covered in detail in the paragraphs below, so we'll concentrate on the remaining key parts of marketing.

Psychographics and Demographics

Google Analytics is a good place to start if you want to learn more about your customers' demographics and psychographics. These figures are used to target your marketing; otherwise, it will be haphazard, hit-or-miss, and ineffective.

Demographics data include information on your consumers' age groups, family backgrounds, level of education, income, and geography. Psychographics can help you understand your consumers' motivations – why are they so interested in the things you sell?

All of these data allow you to create a client profile that describes what makes your potential customers tick. Google Analytics provides a wide range of statistical information, and you may add more to give your marketing efforts the most precise emphasis imaginable.

Reviews & Ratings from Customers

The greatest method to develop trust is to have a feedback page on your website and online store. Humans are notoriously distrustful, and when it comes to shopping online, they have good cause to be. Use this scepticism to your advantage by including a part for client testimonials and ratings, as well as an area where customers can submit evaluations on your products and services.

Potential clients can see the reviews, as well as your responses to them and how you handled any issues. This type of customer connection is the quickest approach to establish trust and demonstrate to them that you are willing to be entirely honest.

Trends in Marketing

Look into marketing methods that are contemporary and well-liked in order to reach the largest possible customer base for your sector.

Private messaging is available on all of the major social media platforms, allowing businesses to communicate with their customers. On all of the social media networks to which you belong, you can have direct conversations with potential customers. Check your social media accounts' private messages on a regular basis and respond to questions as quickly as feasible. This serves as a marketing and customer service channel.

Another marketing strategy to look at is live chat. Users can get help through Shopify's live chat bots, which are available in their extension library.

This solution may not be ideal for a startup that lacks the manpower to handle live chat, but it is something to consider once your company has expanded to the point where it can handle it.

Chat bots are a marketing method that does not necessitate the use of human resources. Customers can get basic queries answered by bots without you having to be there.

Advertisements that appear on the screen

Display advertising are a low-cost marketing strategy that is quite popular. Over the last decade, display advertising has exploded in popularity.

This form of advertising is now lot more targeted at your target audience, and the outcomes are far better than in the past.

There are two ways that display advertising works. You go to the most popular websites in your niche and see if you can buy ad space there. This allows you to advertise to those who are specifically interested in your niche products. The second alternative is to collaborate with a well-known ad network that will take care of your display ad placement.

Instead of reaching a big number of individuals who are not interested in your niche products, the purpose of display ads is to bring your brand to the notice of potential buyers who fall into your niche.

Wherever your niche congregates, be there. Search the internet to find where the people who would be your niche clients congregate. There will be blogs and social media groups wherever there is a niche. Join these groups to learn more about your niche. Examine what they have to say about your specialised products, as well as their requirements and desires.

Because you are not bombarding individuals with your business and advertisements, this is subtle marketing. You are an authority in your field and can answer questions, give advise, and put people in the right direction. Most bloggers and social media groups will gladly accept your ideas, incorporate your posts, and provide credit to your company.

Retarget

According to statistics, up to 98 percent of individuals do not make a purchase the first time they visit a website because they prefer to window shop before making a decision. Rather from becoming discouraged by the low conversion rate for first-time visitors, consider it an opportunity for a new marketing plan.

According to statistics, retargeting clients with display advertisements can increase conversion rates by up to 70%.

For a variety of reasons, retargeting is currently underutilised.

Some companies believe they don't have enough time to retarget potential clients. Many entrepreneurs, particularly those new to the dropshipping company model, are simply unaware of this marketing tactic. This means that now is the best time to start employing retargeting because it will put you ahead of your competitors.

Upsell and cross-sell

Cross-selling and upselling are two of the most effective marketing methods for engaging impulse shoppers, as they are the easiest to persuade to make more than the one purchase they had planned.

Your store and website are silent as a dropshipping business. Your potential clients are not bombarded with eager salespeople offering helpful suggestions on how to upsell or cross sell your products by proposing complementary items. Cross-selling is accomplished by grouping products that complement one another.

There are amazing cross-selling and upselling plugins available regardless of whether you operate an online store on a retail platform or sell directly through your own website. There are a number of Shopify, WooCommerce, and WordPress plugins, as well as standalone plugins, available for this marketing method.

Allow these plugins to be the voice of your company, with unobtrusive pop-ups based on the goods visitors are exploring, alerting them to more products they might be interested in.

Try out a few different upsell and cross-sell plug-ins to see which one best suits your marketing objectives.

Marketing Strategies That Are Expensive

With so many low-cost and cost-effective marketing choices accessible, it isn't necessary to use expensive marketing techniques. If you have the financial means to invest in high-cost marketing, there are two prominent options for you to consider.

Promotions and giveaways have always been popular with businesses of all types, and you can use them to generate a lot of attention to your dropshipping firm. It's worth your time to consider this and see if you can fit it into your budget.

Influencer marketing has emerged as a result of social media. Because of the widespread use of social media, these influencers have a lot of clout, and if any of them recommend your products, it might result in a significant increase in sales. If you're interested in this style of marketing, you should spend some time investigating which social media influencers may be beneficial to your industry.

Branding

Branding is a crucial aspect of a dropshipping business that is frequently overlooked.

Some people believe that having a dropshipping store on Shopify or a listing on one of the online retail platforms is sufficient to have an online presence.

Branding helps your store stand out among the crowd. Without branding, dropshipping on retail platforms makes you invisible.

Yes, creating your own distinct brand takes time and effort; you have the option of being faceless in the crowd or standing out and being noticed. Your retail platform branding and your personal website branding are inextricably linked.

Customers regard you as trustworthy since they can associate your company with your own brand. This is also an excellent marketing tactic.

Because you do not physically stock the products and your suppliers manage storage and delivery, branding for the dropshipping model differs from branding for other retail enterprises.

Your website, your online store on retail platforms, and social media all contribute to your brand. Your goal with branding is to ensure that people know your logo and identify it with your business as far as possible on the internet. Dropshipping has a distinct and personal character thanks to branding.

It's critical to understand that your dropshipping business's branding must develop with it from the outset. Attempting to brand yourself when you have more time or are financially stable does not work effectively. Attempting to retroactively brand yourself does not work effectively. You've lost too much ground because all of your previous consumers have nothing specific to remember you by and will have gone on.

Advertising on Social Media

We all know the significant influence social media has on just about every aspect of people's life, as it began around four decades ago as newsgroups where people could connect. Using social media to promote your company offers you access to a large audience that you can target with your branding and advertising. With ad campaigns and your logo on everything, make your presence known on every possible social media platform.

Using social media as a marketing tool for branding has an additional benefit. Every post you make to your Instagram or Facebook account generates organic traffic at a significantly lesser cost than more traditional marketing methods.

Here's a quick rundown of the advantages of using social media to boost your brand:

Organic traffic at a minimal cost; little competition due to the fact that most businesses ignore social media marketing. The written word does not speak as loudly as pictures do.

Post videos and photographs that pertain to your business and specialty items to offer customers a better understanding of what you're selling. Easy to set up and utilise social media accounts. No or very minimal advertising charges. Although most social media networks provide paid advertising, it is not required.

You can promote effectively on social media and reach a huge audience. You can use sponsored ad campaigns to improve your branding even more if you chose to do so later.

White Labeling is a term used to describe the process of

Everyone is aware of how fiercely competitive the global marketplace has become. White labelling is such a powerful branding approach that Amazon has embraced it and begun offering their own white-labeled products in order to boost earnings.

It's a straightforward notion that works nicely for a dropshipping company. Instead of his own corporate labels, you negotiate with your dropshipping supplier to white label the things you order from him with your own white label and brand. The provider rebrands the product for you and it becomes "your" product by exchanging labelling. Many dropshipping suppliers are pleased to do so because their products are still sold, only under a different name.

For the suppliers, the most crucial thing is that no changes are made to their items, only the labels.

White labelling is an additional marketing strategy.

When your suppliers rebrand your orders, you can ask them to add a packing slip with your contact information, logo, and corporate policies as an extra marketing approach.

Marketing for Packaging and Delivery

Another alternative that will help your branding is to add a booklet or minicatalogue that will introduce customers to more of your products.

Blogging

Blogging is big business these days, and it's an important part of your online presence that may help your dropshipping business in a variety of ways. Consider this: there are currently over 409 million people reading over 23.7 billion pages every month, demonstrating the necessity of having your own blog.

The graph below shows how internet users obtain reliable information from blogs.

2017 (FitSmallBusiness)

It does not require you to be a well-known author or spend hours producing blog entries to be productive. Make it short and entertaining, and relate it to posting on social media on a daily basis. Everyone spends time, and the majority of individuals do so on a daily basis, publishing on various social media platforms about their daily lives.

Blogging is a business asset that allows you to expand your business by simply doing what you already do on social media sites like Facebook and Twitter.

The numerous advantages of blogging can be divided into four groups.

Advantages of SEO

Your website will gain a new page for each blog post you write. This is brand-new, one-of-a-kind information that has never been indexed by search engines before. Your ratings rise with each new blog post, and you become more prominent when people search for your keywords, resulting in more traffic to your website. Freshness of material is one of the characteristics that search engines look for, and blogging keeps the search engines fed.

When search engines crawl your website and find only outdated content, the intervals between crawls grow longer and longer. It keeps them interested if you offer them new content on a frequent basis, and it keeps the search engines checking your website at short intervals.

Maintain the quality of your blog posts by making them informative and engaging. Other bloggers will link to your blog post and reference your content in their own blogs. This creates authoritative links, also known as inbound links. This will improve your SEO and drive more traffic to your website.

When you publish niche-specific pieces with a narrow focus, you can employ long-tailed keywords, which are search phrases that contain many words. Blog entries that focus on the benefits of a specific product or meet a specific consumer demand will produce more traffic from people who are interested in those specific features of the product you offer, which will help your optimization.

Your blog entries offer long-term SEO benefits that last for weeks or months after they've been published, without requiring you to rewrite them.

Advantages for Your Business

The dropshipping business model faces intense competition, and many competitors take the easy way out by looking at what other retailers in the same industry are doing and adapting ideas from these sites for their own store design and marketing.

Make use of your writing talents to highlight elements of your own store that set it apart from others in your niche, as well as specifics about the things you sell. Visitors will remember you if you use these subtle reminders in your blog entries, and they will recognise your store because of your writing. A competitor cannot readily employ this type of blog article, as they could with more generic postings.

Customers consider specialty stores to be those that cater to a specific specialisation and sell all of the things associated with that niche. They believe that if you specialise, you are an authority in that niche and a responsible vendor who understands all of the community's unique concerns, requirements, and desires. They trust your knowledge and input if, for example, your niche is fishing and all the equipment and gadgets related to that niche.

Your blog postings allow you to demonstrate to your customers that you are informed about your topic and a member of that community. One of the finest ways to grow your brand is to write well-thought-out blog content.

Advantages of Marketing

It is not difficult to use your blog to advertise your brand across all social media channels. The rule is to provide readers with high-quality content rather than generic content that they can get elsewhere. Take it a step further by posting links to your blog pieces on your social media sites. Present the information of your blog entries in a variety of eye-catching styles that may also be utilised on other platforms. People adore sharing infographics and instructive or product educational videos, which are two of the most popular forms. This broadens your audience and opens the door to new clients.

Improved Customer Service

People enjoy learning about topics about which they are unfamiliar or desire to learn more. They dislike being scolded because it makes them feel out of control and as if they are back in school.

This is why your blog is so valuable to your company; people enjoy being educated through blogs since it is informal and they are not being lectured.

You can educate your customers about the industry your specialty represents and give them general information about your company and products by writing helpful blog entries. Instead of directly facing your clients with a sales pitch, blog to give them the impression that you are open and honest, and that you care about their needs and wishes.

People prefer reading blog entries to visiting your website's FAQ page. Answer questions on your blog. Making a brief series of articles that address the most common questions clients have regarding products, service delivery, and other topics is a terrific idea.

You show your store and website visitors that you are approachable and ready to keep communication open between your business and your consumers through your blog articles and comments. When visitors post comments, conduct some research on them and respond with positive remarks. You acquire a deeper understanding of your clients' behaviour patterns, which allows you to better design your marketing campaigns.

Chapter Twelve: Optimize Your Website For Sale

For many people, search engine optimization is a terrifying concept. They quickly consider the complexities and technologies involved, as well as the cost of hiring an expert. Yes, SEO is difficult, but once you grasp the fundamentals, the picture becomes more clearer, and everything you need to do makes sense.

For your dropshipping business's website to be seen in search engines, it must be optimised. You'll be unable to earn sales unless you have a decent search ranking that allows you to appear high enough when potential buyers search for your products.

Setting up your website for sales and conversions fall within the category of marketing, therefore it's reasonable that many business owners are perplexed when we talk about optimising your website for sales. Both approaches operate together to attract potential clients to your website and keep them there long enough for a sale to be made.

The most frequently asked question is whether SEO can truly assist in increasing conversion rates. The answer is unmistakably yes. We'll walk you through each stage of the process after you understand why your website needs to be improved.

Make your website a workhorse with these tips.

Conversion rates are currently at 2.5 percent across e-commerce websites, which is not encouraging. This means that having a great-looking website is insufficient. To increase the conversion rate of your website traffic, you must research your niche audience and cater to their requirements and desires. Making your website work as hard as possible is one strategy to increase consumer loyalty. Easy site navigation will provide your visitors with the finest possible client experience.

This is why you must optimise your website because there will be no conversions if your audience cannot find you.

Attend to Your Audience's Expectations

to provide your consumers with what they desire Give customers a cause to want your merchandise if you employ lead magnets. If your niche is outdoor kitchens, for example, visitors will flock to your site because they are looking for a new wood burning stove. When a visitor comes to your website, he is greeted with an in-depth blog entry about the benefits of wood burning stoves and the best models for various situations. This catches his interest right away. You persuade him to sign up for your email list at the end of the post by offering him a downloadable guide with decor ideas and information on which models are best for different sorts of outdoor kitchens.

A few days later, you follow up on the lead magnet with something like a complimentary consultation with a local decor expert. You've met the customer's demands and exceeded his expectations, resulting in a conversion. This scenario applies to any niche products you have and whatever incentives are best appropriate for them.

The key to bringing a customer to your website is optimization, and then your efforts to appeal to your site visitors will earn you a new customer.

Your Website Should Appeal to a Specific Niche Audience

Your purpose and the search engines' goal are identical; the tactics employed are simply different. You must examine the behaviour patterns of customers in your niche, and Google analyses literally millions of websites using over 200 distinct ranking indicators, but your objectives are the same. To provide the best possible experience for your website visitors by providing them with good information and prioritising the contents that provide the most value.

For SEO, you should concentrate on employing semantic keywords, which are the words and phrases used by a search engine user to find what he or she is looking for, also known as search intent. When you optimise your website for sales with the purpose of increasing conversions, you direct visitors to buy your products, subscribe to your email list, or join your social media sites.

When you optimise for both your website goals and SEO, you build a far better working relationship and interaction between the search engines and your website, which leads to increased consumer satisfaction.

When search traffic clicks on one of your sponsored listings or on a paid advertisement, businesses spend a significant amount of money on paid advertising to attract visitors. However, this sort of advertising has a conversion rate of less than 2% on average.

While it is true that developing and promoting your website content requires time, effort, and money, the organic traffic you obtain from SEO is completely free.

Customers who find your website through organic search have a much higher conversion rate, at over 14%.

Investing your time, effort, and money to increase organic traffic to your website takes time, and many individuals are impatient and expect immediate results. Paid advertising produces short-term outcomes, whereas organic traffic produces long-term results with a much higher conversion rate.

Data Analysis on the Internet

The analysis of your website data is the first step in the website optimization process. This allows you to observe patterns in website visitor behaviour that will help you decide where to apply and focus your SEO efforts.

Google Search Console is an excellent tool that provides user behaviour reports, such as tracking key metrics for your bounce rate, number of sessions, and unique sessions of visitors. The behaviour reports show you how your site visitors behave while on your website, which pages they visit the most, and which specific pages lead to the best conversion rates.

Researching Keywords

In the previous decade, search engine optimization has altered dramatically. You can't just pick a few keywords you believe are relevant and run with them, produce an article or two, and expect to be ranked. Today, achieving that coveted top page placement in the search results is a precise science including multiple criteria.

Ubersuggest is a fantastic free keyword research tool for locating keywords related to your niche, specialised items, and business. This tool is excellent for locating long-tail keywords that are relevant to the user intent of your website users and potential clients. You can utilise broad keywords in Ubersuggest and then filter the keyword results in various ways to get long-tail keywords to target, for example, a specific demographic within your specialty.

There are other tools that are similar to Ubersuggest, both free and paid, so check out a few until you discover one that you like best.

Content That Is Beneficial

In previous chapters, we discussed the significance of providing high-value material as well as the advantages that come with it. This is especially true when it comes to SEO and your search engine rating.

Run a search for your principal keyword to determine the appropriate length of your content for optimization. Check the length of the pages in the top ten SERPs results for that specific term. This provides you a decent idea of how long the posts you should focus on should be.

This is crucial since it tells Google that you're offering a lot of content and that users are spending a lot of time on that page, which is good for your search ranking.

Search Engine Optimization (SEO) on the Page

Keep on-page optimization simple and straightforward. The purpose of on-page SEO is to make your website's design, graphics, and text understandable to search engines.

Select a few relevant keywords and use them strategically.

Use a service like Ubersuggest to find a few of the most relevant keywords that define your niche or items. Use the keywords a couple times on each page and make sure they flow smoothly through the material. Keyword cramming on each page will not improve your search rating because search engine algorithms are clever and ignore keyword cramming.

Image Enhancement

Find appropriate ways to use your keywords for image file names and alt tags instead of utilising the generic "image.jpg" to name image files and alt tags. Investing the extra time to properly optimise your photos will help your on-page SEO.

Internal Hypertext Links

Internal links are hyperlinks within a page's text that go to another page on your site with relevant information. Internal links convey page authority to another page, spreading link equity (also known as link juice) across your website. So, if you have some pages that don't rank well, you can use an internal link to connect them to a page that does. Internal links aid in the promotion of pages with lower rankings. Internal links allow search engine spiders to crawl particular pages since they direct them to other pages.

Link Explorer is a terrific tool that takes the guesswork out of internal linking and has a lot of useful features. It's definitely worth getting if you're not sure how to go about building internal links.

Optimization for mobile devices

In the last few years, mobile devices have become the primary method of accessing the internet, as shown in the graph below. As a result, it has become a requirement for websites to be mobile-friendly.

(2019, Perficient Digital)

Since Google released the mobile-first index in 2018, making your website mobile-friendly is a must. You risk losing a big percentage of conversions from mobile internet users if you don't.

Responsive design is the simplest technique to make your website mobile friendly. WordPress removes the burden of coding off your shoulders by providing free and premium themes with built-in responsive design.

Backlinks of Superior Quality

Backlinks are viewed by Google as a measure of your website's legitimacy, and this has an impact on your ranking. The golden criterion for backlinks is that they must come from a trustworthy source. If you have a lot of backlinks but they come from untrustworthy websites, it won't help your ranking. When it comes to earning search engine credibility, quality clearly outweighs quantity.

Obtaining high-quality backlinks necessitates effort on your part, as cultivating trustworthy backlinks requires time and effort. It's worth it since excellent backlinks are SEO gold, and there are so many different ways to gain backlinks that it can be enjoyable rather than a job.

Infographics are one of the most common strategies to obtain backlinks.

Make eye-catching infographics that people will want to share. Guest blogging is another common method of obtaining backlinks. Writing excellent posts for other websites' blogs not only earns you backlinks, but it also exposes your website to new audiences and improves your online reputation.

Donating to nonprofit organisations is an intriguing approach to gain backlinks.

Look for websites in your niche that not only take donations but also link back to the sites from whom they received them.

These are just a few suggestions for obtaining high-quality backlinks; there are many more to consider. Use your imagination to look for link-building chances that fascinate you and are relevant to your niche.

Page loading time

The speed with which your pages load has a significant impact on SEO and the percentage of customers who convert. Shoppers are not willing to wait for a website to load, and over half of all visitors to websites with terrible loading times will abandon their shopping carts.

If the page takes three seconds or longer to load, they will abandon it.

Google implemented a page speed upgrade to their algorithm in 2018, making it vital to ensure that your website loads quickly because it affects your search page ranking.

(2010, Soasta Inc.)

It's not tough to fix your poor page performance and boost your ranking and conversion rate.

Google's Page Speed Insights is the best programme to use to fix this issue. The tool provides a detailed breakdown of your website's loading time on mobile and desktop PCs. The software then gives you step-by-step instructions on how to correct the issues and increase your page loading speed, as well as techniques for reducing server calls, reducing file size, and minimising load time.

Chapter Thirteen: How To Scale Your Dropshipping Business

A dropshipping company's ability to communicate is critical to its success. Your firm will stagnate if it does not grow, and that is the beginning of the end for any business. You must grow your business no matter what your personal ambitions are for it, whether you want to become a business tycoon or just settle in and have a pleasant and sustainable business. Scaling can be intimidating because you'll be stepping outside of your comfort zone and taking on new responsibility. However, if you take it step by step and use all of the tools and tactics at your disposal, expanding your business becomes simple and enjoyable.

Scaling is not a one-size-fits-all approach to expanding your company. It is extremely adaptable, and if one method of scaling does not work for your niche, you have a number of different options to try out and adopt that best suit your dropshipping business. That is why scaling is so great; you can add as many different options as you want, and there are no limitations.

Are you up to the task?

Premature scaling is a term used in business to describe increasing your firm without first laying a solid foundation on which to develop your scaling. This is a trap that not just fledgling firms fall into, but even long-established businesses, and it always leads to failure.

For your scaling efforts to be effective, you must complete the following steps before you may be ready to scale.

2017 (Hackermoon)

Cash Back Guarantee

Prepare a cash reserve for your firm before scaling to account for any setbacks that may occur. This will allow you to switch strategies while scaling and have the funds to fall back on if one method fails.

You won't be able to test multiple strategies to find the optimal product and market match if you don't have a financial reserve.

Taking Reasonable Steps Forward

From the beginning to the end of the scaling process, you must follow the stages in the correct order. Starting at the wrong end of the scale will result in a lot more work, wasted money, and missed chances.

Because you've started investing money on items, hiring a person or individuals to help run the business, and advertising, you'll be less flexible to manoeuvre once you've committed to the scaling process.

It is not difficult to prevent all of the pitfalls associated with early scaling. Spend no money on non-essentials and save all spare cash so you can continue without running out of money in the middle of scaling. Once you've got that in place, double-check that you know exactly what your customers want, that you have all of the ways to reach potential customers, and that you've set up strategies and advertising to reach all of your potential customers in your scaling effort's target group. The final phase is to test any items you wish to scale or new products you want to introduce to your company. Scaling must be based on verifiable test results, not guesswork or what others claim to be the latest trends or fads. Once you've completed all of the above, you've eliminated the risk of early scaling and are ready to begin scaling your dropshipping business.

Vertical Scaling

Traditional vertical scaling entails adding new products to your niche or expanding your specialization's categories. You also boost your advertising budget for existing ad packages that are performing really well. In summary, you expand your ad spend and provide more items, but you don't focus on identifying new customers to target within your niche. This is a tried-and-true method of scaling with a decent track record.

Horizontal Scaling

Horizontal scaling provides you with numerous options, or combinations of horizontal scaling solutions, to apply, whatever fits your business best and is most pleasant for you to utilise. Essentially, rather than expanding upwards with your existing items, you scale broad by presenting them to new consumers.

Become a Franchise Owner

You duplicate your current business and online store in order to sell to customers in your specialty who speak a different language. If you speak more than one language, you can take care of this by simply translating everything on your current website into the target language.

If you don't know another language, form a partnership with someone who does and split the income from the new franchise website 50/50.

Duplicating your business in another language appeals to people in countries where English is not the official language. Europeans, Balkans, and Far Easterners prefer to shop online in their own language and use the Euro as their payment currency.

Duplicating has the advantage of increasing conversion rates, but it also means taking on a lot more work and limiting the number of nations you can target in your scaling efforts.

Keep it English and expand your horizons.

Scaling globally and maintaining everything in English has the disadvantage of losing potential clients who prefer not to do business in English and pay in USD, resulting in a lower conversion rate.

Scale worldwide for nations where English is the official language or one of the official languages to compensate for this disadvantage. This method of global scaling requires far less effort than duplicating your website, allowing you to focus on other aspects of your organisation.

Scaling Into Adjacent Niche

This is a terrific approach to scale your business by looking into niches that are adjacent to your own and seeing if there are any products that will complement the products you are already selling.

Look for things that your niche's clients would be interested in purchasing, and then provide a couple at a time to see how they react. Your sales statistics will clearly show you which products your niche customers prefer, allowing you to alter the products you sell from adjacent niches.

This type of scaling can be done forever without the need for additional advertising until you are certain that any nearby specialised products are feasible to be introduced permanently.

Lookalike Audiences on Facebook

Facebook has a segmentation function that generates lookalike audiences based on your current following. The programme uses your followers' interests and demographics to build a lookalike audience that you may target. Because the demographics and interests of the new audience are so similar to those of your present followers, this method of scaling allows for targeted marketing and identifies groups with a high conversion rate.

Facebook searches its huge user base for commonalities to produce a lookalike audience that would never have been discovered without Facebook's user data. This technique works as long as your client group has at least 100 people, but the larger your total, the more powerful it becomes.

You can select multiple sorts of lookalike audiences by using your customer lists, internet traffic, and fan pages to generate your lookalike audience.

Demographics in Detail

You can further refine your demographics for the lookalike audience by specifying factors such as geographical area, gender, and age group to target your advertisements even more precisely.

Selection of Audience Size

Selecting the large audience option to increase the amount of individuals you contact who are similar to your present audience will give you a lot larger audience, but there will be fewer commonalities shared than there are between your fans and current customers.

When you choose a smaller lookalike audience, the number of people who view your advertising will be less, but those people will have many more traits with your fans and clients.

CBO of Facebook

The campaign budget optimization (CBO) tool, which was released in September 2019, allows you to optimise how your advertising spend is dispersed. This system now optimises your ad budget in real time across all of your ad sets. It focuses on the best chances one at a time, optimising them based on the least expensive cost per result. It goes on to the next best opportunity once it has finished with one. The amount spent on the preceding ad set is not taken into account. The benefit of CBO is that it intelligently optimises your campaign budget to target the advertisements that perform the best and the people that respond the best, so you don't waste money on possibilities that aren't as likely to lead to sales and conversions.

Customer Match and Google Similar Audiences

Google provides a number of tools to help you re-engage customers and grow your business.

Customer Match uses data that customers have provided with you, both offline and online, to help you re-engage customers across Display, YouTube, Search, Gmail, and Shopping. This tool can also be used to find new clients who are similar to the ones you already have.

Google's Similar Audiences feature works in the same way as Facebook's Lookalike service. Similar Audiences searches frequently leverage your marketing lists, first-party data information, and the interests of your best-performing website visitor groups to target new people who share similar qualities.

Calculate and Plan

It is critical to plan ahead in order to scale successfully. You must perform two unique forecast evaluations in order to be able to plan accurately. To get the most realistic results, you should be as thorough as possible using as many data as feasible.

A customer growth prediction, broken down into categories and broken down by months, including data such as the amount of new clients and projected orders.

An expense projection based on the processes you have in place and will need to cope with the increased amount of orders, comparable to the revenue growth forecast. Also, what infrastructure adjustments will be required, what technological upgrades will be required, and how much extra staff would be required to run the business throughout the scaling time.

Suppliers

Suppliers are an important element of growing your business. You must be able to trust that your suppliers will be able to expand with you, and that you will not be stuck dealing with a supplier that cannot keep up with your increased orders in the middle of your scaling operation. Make sure your supplier can keep up, especially if you're scaling up specialised items or launching new products. If you have any questions about the supplier's ability, you should look for a new or backup supply.

When you start communicating with your suppliers on a larger scale, you're bringing them into the picture. Suppliers are well aware of the advantages that scaling will bring to their company. They'd rather you stay with them, so bargain for the greatest deals on the things you're scaling. The majority of your suppliers will be willing to negotiate if you have established a great business connection with them.

Support Workers As your business expands and orders increase, you'll need support staff because you won't be able to manage all of the orders, client inquiries, and order placement on your own. A negative connection with clients, especially new clients, is something that no firm can afford. You must have a competent individual or persons in place to assist you in dealing with client inquiries, as well as communicating with and placing orders with your suppliers.

Outsourcing by employing a virtual assistant or virtual assistants for your specific business requirements is a cost-effective method to have the appropriate support staff in place. You don't have to pay for things like office space or equipment because you may train and introduce your virtual assistant to your suppliers. This implies you can put the money in your cash reserve to better use in your company.

Automation and Technology

Automation is essential for the seamless operation of any dropshipping business, and this is especially true during the scaling phase. There is just no time to execute jobs manually since they are too time consuming, leaving you with little or no time to focus on the numerous additional tasks required to expand successfully.

Automate order fulfilment and auto order tracking are two types of automation to put in place before you start scaling. These two automated methods keep orders flowing and clients pleased by allowing them to follow the status of their orders. When dealing with first-time consumers who may be wary of working with a company they are unfamiliar with, tracking is very useful.

To avoid communication issues, make sure to integrate as many of your systems as feasible. The more unintegrated systems you have, the more likely they will not work well together, therefore avoid difficulties down the road by integrating your systems as much as feasible.

Chapter Fourteen: Pitfalls And Mistakes To Avoid

We've saved this piece for last because it's the most important. This isn't a doom-and-gloom chapter; it's a go-to part that you'll come back to when problems arise. Everything we discuss here is intended to assist you in navigating the inevitable obstacles you will encounter while starting your own dropshipping business, as well as how to avoid falling into the traps that so many other dropshippers have fallen into before you.

People aren't stupid, thus dropshipping firms don't fail. When you first start out, everyone wants to succeed, which puts a lot of pressure on you.

People commit errors because they are impatient to achieve and adopt shortcuts that lead to disaster. The most common causes of failure in a dropshipping business are a lack of knowledge about what to look for and what to avoid.

The most important thing to remember about this chapter is that others have made these mistakes before you, and some have given up or lost money as a result. They've been there, done that, and you can learn from their experiences. This chapter will assist you in effectively navigating the complex maze of e-commerce.

Failure to Learn from Mistakes

You are a human being, and you will make errors. The most common blunder made by entrepreneurs is failing to learn from their mistakes.

Nobody begins off knowing everything there is to know about dropshipping; you learn as you go along, and you learn from your failures. When a problem arises, you look for remedies and strategies to avoid repeating the same error. You set your dropshipping business up for failure if you refuse to learn or make an attempt to figure out how to fix problems and blunders.

Clients, Audience

You need to know what your market is before you start your dropshipping business. It is a fallacy to believe that having products that are in line with the latest trend would automatically result in success. You must have a precise understanding of who your target audience is; guessing is an expensive mistake. The importance of research cannot be overstated; you must collect statistical data on your niche audience and learn everything you can about them.

We explored cross-selling and upselling as market strategies in Chapter 12. Many dropshipping businesses continue to make the mistake of not upselling. If you don't get to know your target customer well enough to upsell, your profit margin will be constrained. Prepare an upselling strategy and don't rely solely on your front-end products to earn revenue. Upselling is a considerably more cost-effective marketing strategy because these products are not advertised.

You must value your past clients in order to bring in actual money for your company. You've already established a connection and a sale; failing to maintain touch via your email lists is a significant error. Do not solely focus on acquiring new clients; maintaining contact with existing consumers accounts for a significant portion of your overall profit margin.

When starting a dropshipping business, one of the most common mistakes newcomers make is attempting to take on the entire world. You must first learn to walk before you can run, therefore concentrate on your target market in the United States.

Get to know your target audience in the United States, where you have a large specialised audience and can ship quickly and reliably. After you've established your US market and accumulated experience, you might consider expanding internationally.

The website structure, as well as poorly updated product descriptions and names, are two common blunders with reference to the dropshipping company shop and website.

Prospective shoppers are quickly turned away from stores and websites that are not properly and logically set up. Not everyone knows how to code and use HTML, and not everyone has access to a solution. Shopify includes all of the tools and plugins needed to put up a successful business, while the Woocommerce plugin for the WordPress platform is accessible for more experienced entrepreneurs.

Product names and descriptions must be modified in dropshipping businesses that use online platforms such as Alibaba and Aliexpress and employ plugins to import products to their shop and website. The descriptions and product names are irrelevant to your dropshipping business; they need to be changed to focus on your target market.

SEO

Despite all of the available information about search engine optimization and the essential role it plays in a company's online exposure and conversion rate, this remains a major issue. Any area of SEO that is ignored has a long-term detrimental impact on your organisation. Use the many apps and plugins available if you don't think you'll be able to do it alone.

The two most common niche blunders are choosing a niche without conducting extensive research into it and choosing a niche that is overly broad. When you don't do your study, you're more likely to pick the wrong specialty once you've set up and branded your store. This is a costly error because you will have to start again from the beginning. When you can't employ exact and focused keywords, choosing a too broad specialty is catastrophic for marketing, promotions, and SEO.

Brand Recognition

Your dropshipping company's brand visibility is just as crucial as any other retailer's. It's a mistake not to make your brand as apparent as possible at all times. Simple, yet effective, ways to keep your brand visible include bespoke external packaging, a thank you note following delivery, and sending out customer satisfaction surveys.

Customer Service Poor customer service can completely derail your business. Consumers and future customers must come first, and failing to respond quickly and efficiently to customer complaints, queries, and concerns will mark your firm as one to avoid, particularly on social media.

Expectations that are unrealistic

Many startup businesses have failed because they entered dropshipping with the unrealistic expectation of quick money with little or no effort. Enter the company with your eyes wide open. The recipe for success is to know how to promote your products, who your target audience is, how to compete with the many competitors out there, and to be willing to put in the effort.

A common blunder is believing that after you've set up your online business and developed a website, that's all there is to it and you'll start earning passive money. If you don't do anything, that's exactly what you'll get: nothing.

If you don't see instant results or if a strategy fails, you should give up. There is no such thing as immediate success or failure in business; it requires perseverance and patience to succeed.

Not being able to take bad customer comments on social media sites, in your store, or on your website. Negative feedback is not a personal attack; every firm receives it; it does not imply that yours is a failure. Work through the negative feedback, come up with a solution, and then move on.

Goods with a Trademark

Many dropshipping businesses have failed due to selling trademarked products. The trademark regulations in the United States and the European Union are so severe and zealously enforced that losing everything you've fought for, plus the risk of being sued, is simply not worth it.

Suppliers

When an entrepreneur feels happy with a supplier who has provided good service over time, they become overly reliant on that source.

Anything can happen, including stock shortages, large price rises, or a surge in orders that the provider is unable to deliver.

Even if your niche is narrowly focused, it is prudent to have a backup supply.

Marketing

The most common reason dropshipping companies employ inadequate marketing methods is that they do not have a thorough understanding of their specialised clients. As a result, instead of focusing on their particular clientele, their marketing is promoted to everyone.

Another blunder is promoting their products at random rather than investigating the channels where the majority of their clients are active. The results of random marketing are average at best, with very low returns.

Taxes and Legal Liabilities

Legal liabilities are a common hazard for startups, and many people try to avoid them. To avoid legal ramifications, establish your dropshipping firm as a corporation. All agreements, contracts, and business relationships are the responsibility of the firm, not you personally, once you have been officially registered as a business.

Sales tax can be perplexing and lead to a slew of errors. Shopify and Woocommerce include settings that automatically collect sales taxes required on products for merchants who build shops on their platforms.

Order Processing

It's easy to slip into the trap of manually completing orders when you're first starting out, and many people do. This works great in the beginning, but as the business grows, they will be unable to keep up. Use an app like Oberlo to automate your order fulfilment and save yourself a lot of time.

When people purchase online, they make mistakes such as changing their minds about which goods they want or wanting to cancel an order. To ensure client satisfaction, it is your responsibility to ensure that this procedure is performed appropriately and professionally. Make sure your supplier verifies any modifications with you, and then check with the client that the adjustments were done, or the correct reimbursements will be applied.

CONCLUSION

You now have everything you need to start your dropshipping business. Begin small and aim high. You're aware of what to look out for and what to avoid. Many people have a ghoulish desire to give uninvited advice to entrepreneurs by relating horror stories of failure and money wasted by beginning a dropshipping business. Do not pay attention to them.

It takes time to build a dropshipping business; it does not happen overnight. When your biggest investment is in yourself, success will follow. Your time, effort, determination, and desire to achieve are all valuable assets.

When you first start, it's natural to feel overwhelmed. But keep in mind that every stride you take is a step ahead. The most challenging aspect of starting a dropshipping business is getting started. It doesn't matter if you're unsure about something; most individuals are terrified about starting a business.

If you get off to a good start, you've already won half the battle. Think carefully and don't rush into things, only to have to go back and correct your mistakes afterwards.

Use every tool at your disposal to fully utilise all of the capabilities of the dropshipping software that best suits your niche.

Despite all of the doomsayers who claim that dropshipping is not a viable business strategy, it is extremely popular.

Remember that Jeff Bezos and Bill Gates both started in their garages, with computer wires all over the place and a scrawled banner on the wall with their firm name.